SUN LIFE
STRATEGY FOR MANAGING THE NATURA 2000 NETWORK IN UMBRIA

Life13 NAT/IT/371

SUN LIFE is one of 12 Italian projects financed in 2013 by the European Commission's LIFE+ Nature & Biodiversity Programme to initiate policies regarding nature and biodiversity and to favour the development of the Natura 2000 Network.

Coordinating partner:

Umbria Region

Associated partners:

Comunità Ambiente

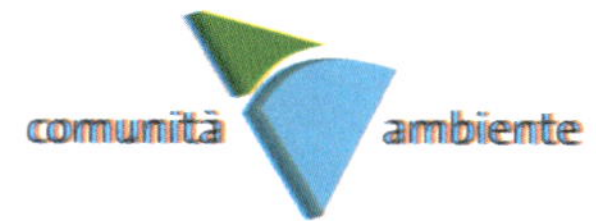

University of L'Aquila

University of Camerino

University of Perugia

The present volume was created and edited by UNICAM as established in action E5 (Paolo Perna, Ilenia Pierantoni, Andrea Renzi, Massimo Sargolini).

INDEX

1
INTRODUCTION

Massimo Sargolini, Paolo Perna, Andrea Renzi

SAAD School of Architecture and Design – UNICAM University of Camerino

The SUN LIFE – Strategy for the Natura 2000 Network in the Umbria Region – LIFE13 NAT/IT/000371 is a project financed by the European Community within the LIFE+2013 Funding Programme.

The main objective of the project is to respond to the need to conserve the Natura 2000 Network by adopting a strategic approach that involves the entire territory of the Umbria Region. This is done by creating the basic elements necessary to develop, in a medium-long-term perspective, the ability to manage biodiversity in close connection with the various uses and transformation of the land, the related socioeconomic activities, and a campaign to increase awareness and knowledge about the protection of environmental resources.

To correctly address such a broad, systemic vision, numerous partners have come together to define the project. In addition to the Umbria Region, which played a leading role, participants include the Universities of L'Aquila (Department of Civil, Construction-Architectural, and Environmental Engineering), Camerino (School of Architecture and Design), and Perugia (DCBB – Department of Chemistry, Biology, and Biotechnology and DSA3 – Department of Agrarian, Food, and Environmental Sciences), and Comunità Ambiente.

In its definition of preparatory actions that anticipated a draft of the strategy, the project placed particular emphasis on appropriately assessing the strong and weak points of the existing planning system. This was done to provide a framework of reference capable of supporting each decision-making process tied to the planning and management of existing regulatory measures (on the different levels of government) and to estimate the socioeconomic value of the Natura 2000 Network. At the same time, with these basic considerations, policies and strategies were developed to identify the professional fields revolving around the Natura 2000 Network.

The strategy proposed by the SUN LIFE Project implemented an integrated and coordinated management system for the Natura 2000 Network in Umbria, introducing new measures to manage, conserve, and enhance biodiversity and the landscape, in line with the 2020 Biodiversity Strategy and the European Landscape Convention.

This publication follows the path taken over the four years of the SUN LIFE project. The first part traces the construction of the cognitive framework, which is composed of investigations into the state of biodiversity, analyses of the interferences in planning (on the local and supralocal scales) with the existing plans and measures for management of the Natura 2000 Network, and thematic studies on the ecosystem services and green professions. In the second part, the strategy, the main output of the project, is investigated with respect to its methodological and thematic aspects. The other tools made available by the Umbria Region are also described, such as the new PAF (Priority Action Framework), the guidelines for operators in the sector (farmers and foresters), and the projects to support professions related to the protection and enhancement of biodiversity. Finally, in the same section, the two pilot projects presented in the June 2018 LIFE call are presented. In the last two sections, the themes of monitoring and communication of the project are described.

1.1

Project objectives

Livia Bellisari, Oliviero Spinelli

Comunità Ambiente

The Natura 2000 Network in Umbria is composed of 102 sites: 5 SPAs (according to avifauna species) and 97 SACs. The regional Network also encompasses 41 habitats of European interest, of which 11 are defined as primary for their particular importance, 143 animal species (4 primary), and 8 species of plants. The Natura 2000 Network covers about 15% of the entire regional territory.

The main objective of the SUN LIFE project is to define a management strategy for the entire regional Network to guarantee its effective, long-lasting management by achieving and maintaining a favourable state of habitat and species conservation. Measures for conservation, the restoration of connectivity, and ecological functionality, as well as the related possible sources of European, national, and regional financing are identified. The strategy aims to experiment with integrated, unitary, and coordinated management of the Network, introducing both new measures to manage, conserve, and regenerate the landscape in application of the European Landscape Convention, and measures suitable for pursuing balanced development of "green" jobs and tourism compatible with the conservation of habitats and protected species.

This integration seems vital considering that:

- the fragmentation of the territory, landscape patchwork, and ecological functions represents a transverse threat for species, habitats, and ecosystems disturbed by current climate change. It is addressed in a broad scale of intervention, with forms of territorial government that consider the territory in its entirety;
- the conservation of biodiversity and the success of the Natura 2000 Network are based on a balanced relationship between the environment and the social and economic needs of the people that live there, with regard for sustainable development;
- it is necessary to efficiently use the available funds, drawing on all resources made available in the various sectors tied to the Natura 2000 Network in an integrated, coordinated way.

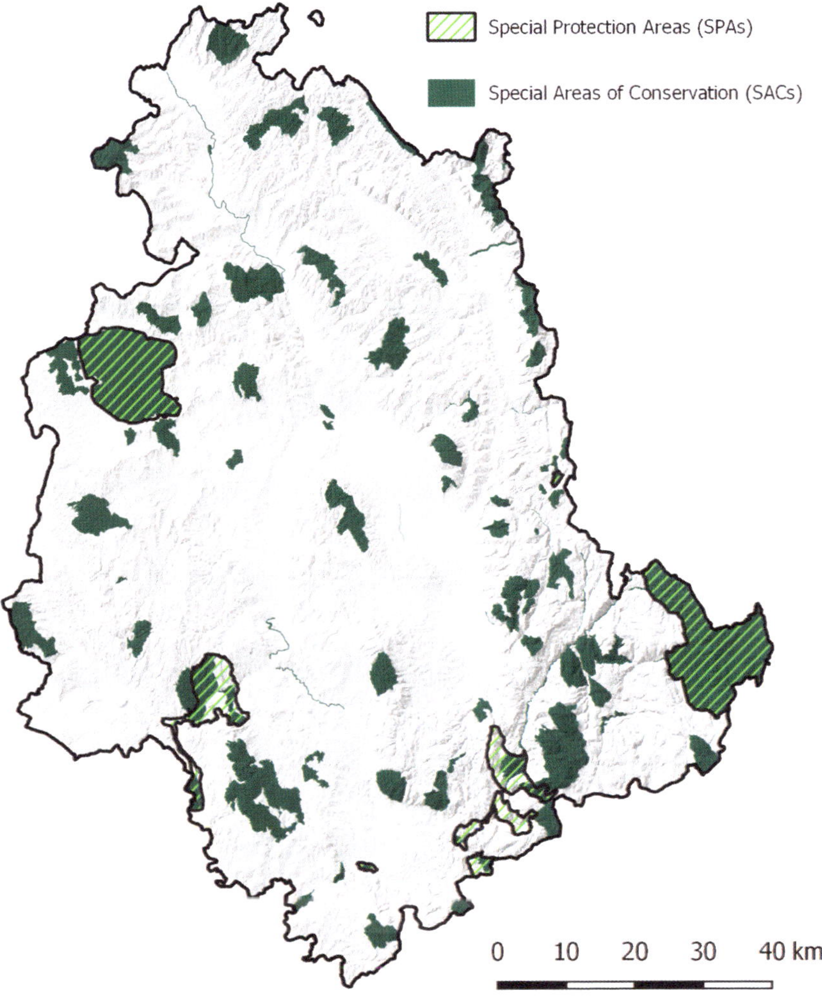

Fig.1 Natura 2000 Network in Umbria Region

Rather than establishing concrete actions for conservation, the project developed a strategy to manage the Natura 2000 Network in Umbria, which aims to favour conservation, landscape regeneration, and social development, thereby affecting the entire territory.

The definition of this strategy aims to achieve the following results:
* guarantee efficient, integrated management of the regional Natura 2000 Network;
* produce a realistic overview of the value of the Natura 2000 Network in Umbria, not only from the point of view of conserving nature and in terms of ecosystem services, but also from the socioeconomic point of view;
* spread greater public awareness of the benefits of the Natura 2000 Network and ecosystem services by developing a communication campaign for the greater public, the various stakeholders, and schools;
* involve all interested sectors and civil society in managing the Network through public consultation and the involvement of interest holders, as well as guiding documents specifically developed for farmers and foresters;
* increase the number of green jobs to encourage effective sustainable development of the territory;
* provide a contribution to reach the objectives of the EU strategy for biodiversity in order to pursue the main objective of the EU, to "halt the loss of biodiversity and the degradation of ecosystem services in the EU by 2020, and restoring them in so far as feasible, while stepping up the EU contribution to averting global biodiversity loss";
* put into practice the principles of the European Landscape Convention and the Pan-European Biological and Landscape Diversity Strategy, which aim to ensure that the ecosystems species depend on continue to function, and that biodiversity and landscape conservation is pursued through an integrated framework.

To reach these objectives, numerous activities have been performed in the SUN LIFE project.
As preparatory activities useful to organizing the work and analysis of the content, the partners:
* created an integrated Natura 2000 Network group that included and involved members from the different regional departments;
* analysed and assessed the means of managing the Natura 2000 Network sites in Umbria;
* estimated the socioeconomic value of the regional Natura 2000 Network;
* analysed the "green jobs" connected to the regional Natura 2000 Network.

Following these activities, the working group proceeded with the creation of:
* the management strategy for the Natura 2000 Network;
* a financial plan to manage the Natura 2000 Network in Umbria;
* a review and update of the Priority Action Framework;
* a plan to scientifically monitor all the habitats and species of European interest present in the sites in the regional Natura 2000 Network;
* a guide to identify projects to support the necessary professions to manage and enhance the Natura 2000 Network;
* two guidelines for farmers and foresters to conserve biodiversity in the Natura 2000 Network;
* two pilot projects to respond to management emergencies identified in the regional Priority Action Framework.

These activities were tested with a series of initiatives to communicate and publish the information, such as:

- an informational campaign regarding the value of the Natura 2000 Network through the creation of a project website, the production and distribution of specially designed flyers, and a guide to Natura 2000 Network sites;
- a series of workshops organized for public consultation and to involve interest holders;
- a series of meetings and guided visits aimed at communication, awareness-raising, and information in schools with teachers and students;
- a series of workshops in high schools to raise awareness and educate students about career opportunities deriving from green professions.

The activities performed under the SUN LIFE project therefore contributed to increasing the ability to manage the regional Natura 2000 Network, while raising awareness about and involving citizens in themes of common interest.

1.2

Methodological path to reach the objectives

Livia Bellisari, Oliviero Spinelli

Comunità Ambiente

The SUN LIFE project presents a rather complex organization of objectives and products. For this reason, it was necessary, even in the initial phases, to adopt structures and tools capable of facilitating collaboration and consistency among the various activities.
The coordination tools established in the project were primarily embodied by the Directing Committee and the Natura 2000 Network Group. The Directing Committee mainly brought together the technical managers of each partner, the project manager, and the coordinator. The scope of the Committee, which met periodically, was to provide directions and coordinate the projects, supervise the progress of the activities, plan actions, make shared strategic decisions, and resolve possible difficulties in a concerted manner. The Natura 2000 Network Group, both during the project and after its conclusion, guaranteed the integration of the Umbria Natura 2000 Network management strategy in the various regional policies and facilitated dialogue among the various departments participating in the work. To guarantee consistency and coordination among the different actions aimed at pursuing the project objectives, the partners, with the contribution of the Umbria Region, was organized into working groups.

Thanks to the SUN LIFE project, the Umbria Region has been able to rely on the technical support of a highly qualified partnership under various skills, which can partially be summarized as follows.

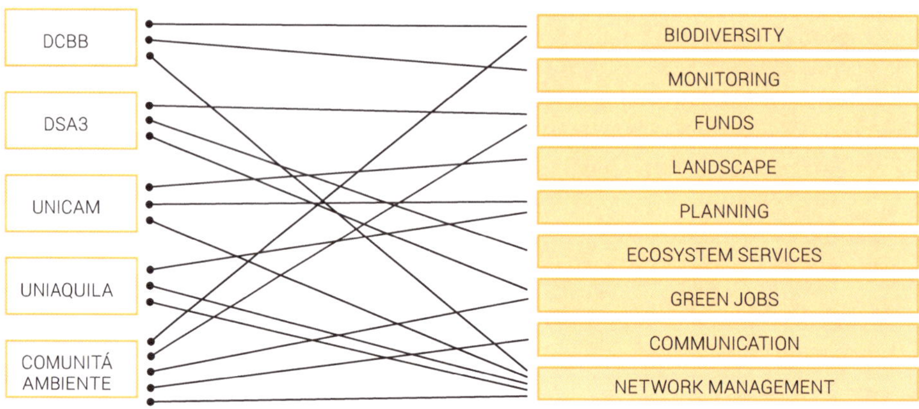

These skills and professions, capitalized on in the project, allowed all the established objectives to be reached. The Umbria Region therefore acquired planning tools to ensure the correct management of the sites in order to improve the conservation of habitats and species of European importance. These strategic tools consider the need for the socio-economic development of the territory and place biodiversity at the centre of a project to renew rural and marginal areas in the Region.

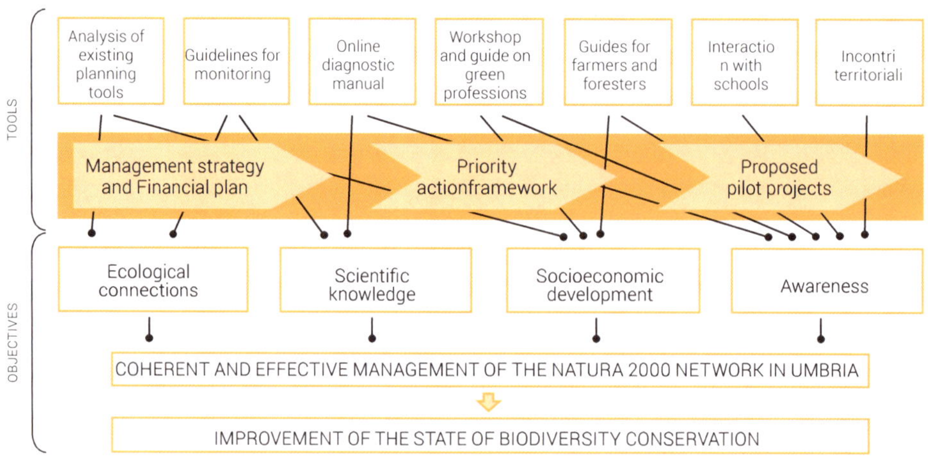

In particular, the management strategy, financial plan, Priority Action Framework, and pilot projects were strongly interconnected and synergistic.

The management strategy defines the objectives to pursue in order to experiment with integrated, unitary, and coordinated management of the Network by reaching and maintaining a favourable state of conservation of habitats and species, renewing ecological connectivity and functionality, and encouraging balanced development of "green" occupation and tourism. The strategy's financial plan identifies available sources of European, national, and regional financing that can be strategically used to reach the objectives.

The Priority Action Framework identifies which of the objectives listed in the strategy are most important, in terms of both urgency and prerequisites with respect to the others.

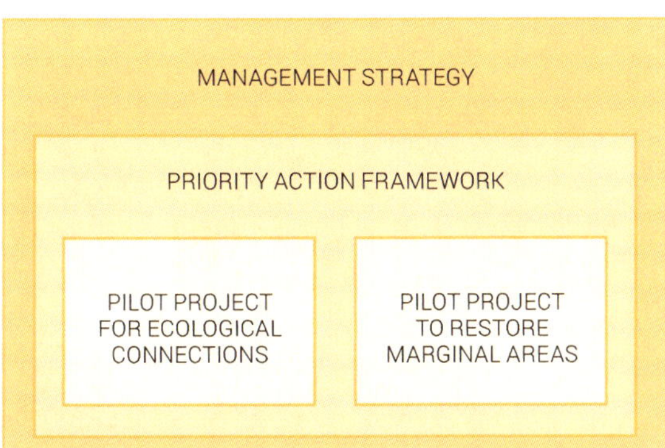

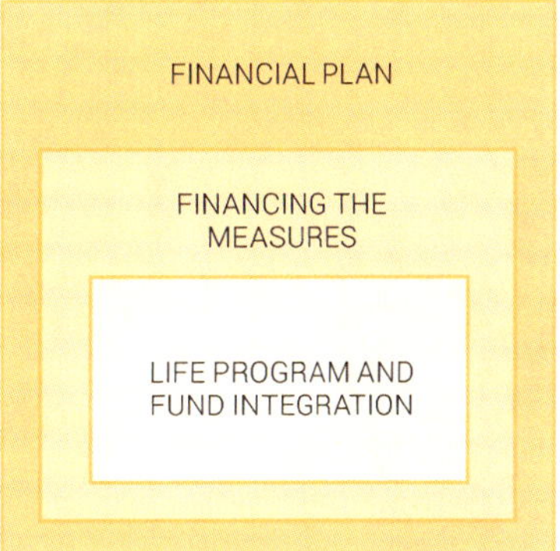

To contribute to reaching some of the priority objectives, the partnership developed two specific planning proposals that respond to: the need to facilitate and increase ecological connections among natural areas to ease, for example, the movement of animals, and guarantee the consistency of the Network; the need to renew marginal areas affected by abandonment, aggravated by the earthquakes in 2016, by constructing a virtuous model of biodiversity conservation and the socioeconomic renewal in the territories.

These planning proposals, if approved, will be financed under the LIFE Programme, but other available funds that can synergically favour the results' achievement will also be mobilized.

2
COGNITIVE FRAMEWORK

2.1

Consistency and state of conservation of the species and habitats in Annexes I, II, IV, and V in Umbria

Daniela Gigante, Enzo Goretti, Gianandrea La Porta, Massimo Lorenzoni, Fabio Maneli, Matteo Pallottini, Laura Pompei, Manuela Rebora, Roberto Venanzoni

Department of Chemistry, Biology, and Biotechnology, University of Perugia

Cristiano Spilinga, Francesca Montioni, Silvia Carletti, Emi Petruzzi

Studio Naturalistico Hyla

One of the cornerstones of Dir. 92/43/EEC (HD), an element of primary importance for management of the Natura 2000 Network, is achieving a favourable state of conservation (SC) for all Habitats[1] (Annex I HD) and species (Annexes II and IV HD) of European interest. The reference parameters for defining the SC as favourable are reported within the HD itself, in Art. 1(e) and 1(i). The Directive establishes the obligation to periodically assess the SC of species and Habitats of European interest, their trends, and future perspectives, and therefore assess the effectiveness of the interventions for protection initiated by the European Union member states.

To provide an overview based on current knowledge of the SC of Habitats and species in the Umbria Natura 2000 Network, data contained within the Natura 2000 Network Standard Data Forms (SDF) were used; these can be consulted through the EEA database (http://natura2000.eea.europa.eu/rdf/ Natura2000_sites.rdf). The values used were those attributed to the parameters related to the "Criteria to evaluate the site for an animal or plant species in Annexes II, IV, and V" and "Criteria to evaluate the site for a given type of natural Habitat in Annex I", as defined by the European Commission (2011).

The values attributed to each species and Habitat in each site were grouped by category (A, B, C, D) and counted. Figures 1–3 show the distribution of the values for each parameter considered, with reference to the different taxonomic groups.

The criteria to evaluate the site for a given animal or plant species in Annexes II, IV, and V were the following (source: European Commission, 2011):

---

1. In the text, "Habitat" will be capitalized to indicate the habitats included in Annex I of Directive 92/4

POPULATION (size and density of the population of the species present in the site compared to the populations present in the national territory).

CONSERVATION (degree of conservation of the important elements of the habitat for the species in question and possibility of restoration).

ISOLATION (degree of isolation of the population present in the site with respect to the natural distribution of the species).

OVERALL ASSESSMENT (overall evaluation of the site's value for the conservation of the species in question).

The criteria used to evaluate a site for a given type of natural Habitat in Annex I are the following (source: European Commission, 2011).

REPRESENTATIVENESS (degree of representativeness of the type of natural habitat in the site)

RELATIVE SURFACE AREA (surface area of the site covered by this type of natural habitat with respect to the total surface area covered by this type of natural habitat in the national territory)

STATE OF CONSERVATION (degree of conservation of the structure and functions of the type of natural habitat in question and the possibility of restoration).

OVERALL ASSESSMENT (overall evaluation of the site's value for the conservation of the natural habitat in question).

In order to present a synthetic treatise, the territory of Umbria was divided into three large ecosystem categories corresponding to well-differentiated territorial/landscape areas affected by different types of land use and human presence:

- Wet areas, encompassing rivers and floodplains, lakes, basins creeks, streams, canals, marshes, ponds, springs, and other bodies of water,
- Plain and plain-hilly landscapes corresponding to the territory between 100 and 600–700 m in altitude,
- Apennine agricultural/forest/pasture landscapes, corresponding to the hilly and mountainous territory between about 600–700 and 2450 m in altitude.

This division allowed all the Habitats and species present in the Umbria Natura 2000 Network to be considered, emphasizing the contexts in which they are most threatened and providing an assessment that appropriately and consistently relates to conservation. Below, a synthetic framework related to the SC of Habitats and species is presented, with reference to this zoning.

Habitats in Annex I

To varying degrees, the Habitats in wet zones (Habitats 3130, 3140, 3150, 3170*, 3240, 3260, 3270, 3280, 3290, 6420, 6430, 6510, 7210*, 7220*, 7230, 91E0*, 92A0), present criticalities related to a high level of fragmentation, strong isolation, and lack of connection, structural simplification, and a high rate of contrast with surrounding areas (generally anthropized). In some cases, this leads to a strong contraction and/or rarefaction of the surface areas, which affect the distribution, structure, and functions with a consequent reduction in the quality of plant communities. For this group of habitats, the SC is mostly inadequate or even poor, while in many cases, as indicated by the representative parameter, they are well represented within the sites in Umbria.

With regard to the Habitats related to the sectors of the plains and low hills (Habitats 4030, 6420, 6510, 91L0, 91M0, 91AA*), the aspect that most affects the SC is the degree of fragmentation, which leads to high levels of contrast with the surrounding areas (generally strongly anthropized). Especially in the plain sectors, the great fragmentation determines the rarefaction of the Habitats, influencing their distribution and modifying their structure and functions, generally degrading the quality of plant communities, reducing the surface area and number of connections, and simplifying the structure. Of the Habitats listed above and present within the plain sites in the Umbria Region, the forested ones (91AA*, 91L0, 91M0 in the case of oak biocenoses) and those tied to mowable grasslands (6510) present an inadequate or poor SC. In particular, their development is drastically reduced, even though the territory presents good potential for these types of Habitat.

The Habitats tied to the Apennine sectors, and the high-hill and mountainous elevations of Umbria in general (Habitats 4060, 4090, 5110, 5130, 5330, 6110*, 6170, 6210 (*), 6220*, 6230*, 6510, 8130, 8210, 8310, 91M0, 9210*, 9260, 9340, 9540), are characterized by a good SC within the sites where traditional agricultural/forestry/pasture activities are practised. In sites where these activities are progressively being abandoned or have ceased entirely, the Habitats show more or less marked levels of degradation, depending on when the activities stopped. All these Habitats, with the sole exception of rocky and forested lands, are affected to varying degrees by natural evolutionary dynamics and therefore by spontaneous recolonization by successive stages of vegetation, which, in the absence of adequate management measures, lead to the development of plant communities different from the original ones that cannot often be found in any Habitat in Annex I. The current surface areas of these Habitats, while in some cases broad and with high values with respect to the parameters of related surfaces, present widespread and evident decline tied to natural successional processes that have led to a visible change, regression, and reduction in the flora. At the same time, some sites show cases where new plant communities can be located in other types of Habitats in Annex I (e.g., 4060, 4090, 5130, etc.). This leads to the pressing problem of prioritizing the different types of Habitat, which is necessary to identify and direct appropriate management measures. With regard to the forest Habitats, these generally show a good SC, while presenting various problems and a varying degree of impact deriving from the use of forestry, which can sometimes simplify the flora in and structure of the plant communities. One strain created on the Habitats located near important plant community limits, for example 9210*, can be ascribed to climate change, which is reflected in the distribution of species and plant communities, altering the composition of the flora.

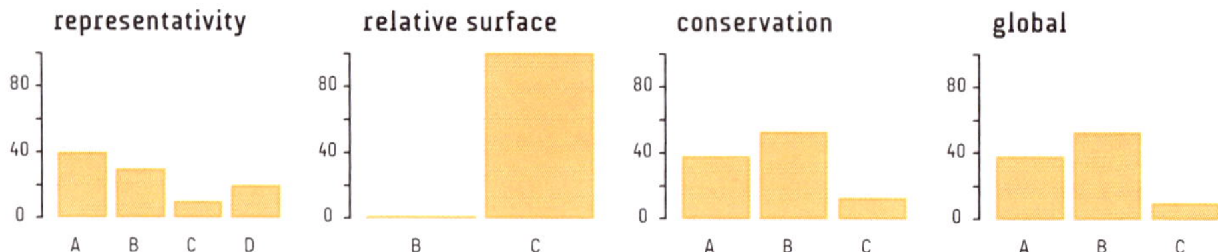

Fig.1 Graphical summary of frequency data for sites in Umbria for the categories of judgement for each assessment criterion used for the Habitats in Annex I, in accordance with the Natura 2000 Network Standard Data Form (European Commission, 2011).

Plant species in Annexes II, IV, and V HD

Within the Natura 2000 Network sites in Umbria, only information related to the species Himantoglossum adriaticum H. Baumann and Jonopsidium savianum (Caruel) Ball ex Arcang. (Annexes II and IV) were reported. However, data related to the presence and distribution of other plant species in Umbria included in the Annexes of the HD are also known. In addition to the above-mentioned species, these include Adonis distorta Ten. (Annexes II and IV), Galanthus nivalis L. (Annex V), Gentiana lutea L. (AnnexV), Iris marsica Ricci & Colasante (Annex IV), and Ruscus aculeatus L. (Annex V). In addition, *Klasea lycopifolia (Vill.) A. & D. Löve (Annexes II and IV), a priority species, is not indicated in any site in the Umbria Natura 2000 Network, although its presence is known and documented at at least two stations in Umbria (Gigante et al., 2014) and it was also reported in the manual for national monitoring of plant species (Ercole et al., 2016).

For the species inserted within the SDFs, based on existing knowledge, the data reported cannot be considered exhaustive with respect to the real situation. With regard to Himantoglossum adriaticum, the reported population data highlight how within the sites, the species population is insignificant, while for Jonopsidium savianum, the populations reach a density of 2%, with high degrees of isolation and an excellent habitat SC, for an overall excellent assessment.

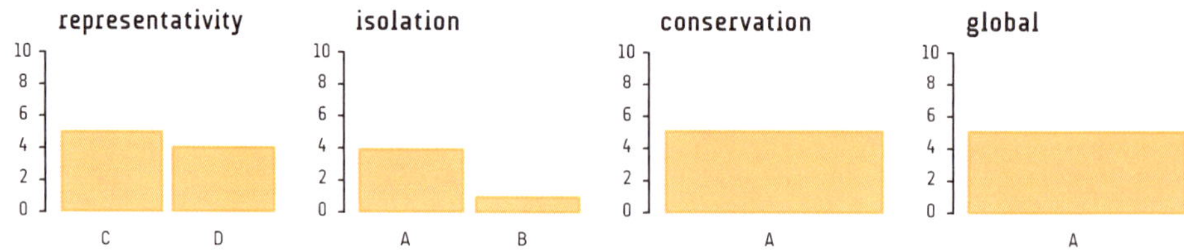

Fig.2 Graphical summary of frequency data for sites in Umbria for the categories of judgement for each assessment criterion used for the plant species in Annexes II, IV, and V in accordance with the Natura 2000 Network Standard Data Form (European Commission, 2011).

Animal species in Annexes II, IV, and V HD and Annex I BD

In general, the SC of fauna of European interest present within the Natura 2000 Network sites in Umbria oscillates between inadequate and poor, with some cases of groups of species or individual species with an inadequate or favourable SC. The general considerations, however, show a non-uniform distribution of data influenced by population data that is either totally lacking, as in the case of birds, or where the population data of nearly all species is labelled "insignificant", as in the case of reptiles.

Invertebrates. Invertebrate populations in the sites in Umbria generally represent between 0 and 2% of the national population (C). For some species, the discovery of individual examples has not allowed for the identification of real populations and only subsequent monitoring will be able to ascertain if their contribution is significant. The SC of the habitat elements is good (B) in most cases, with some exceptions that would require recovery projects, while the degree of isolation of the populations is rather low (C). In effect, only in two cases are largely isolated (A) populations observed, and in one case, the species is found at the edges of the distribution area (B). Overall, the judgement that can be made about the value the sites hold for the conservation of species in this group is good (B). During recent monitoring, additional species of European interest have been discovered, both within and outside the Natura 2000 Network sites, meriting further investigation to assess the SC of the related populations.

Fish and agnatha. Within the SDFs of the Natura 2000 Network sites in Umbria, information is reported regarding only 8 of the 11 species effectively found in the Region. Salmo macrostigma and Barbus plebejus (Annexes II and V) are not indicated in any site in the SDFs, although their presence in the Region is known and documented, while Lethenteron zanandreai is not included in the SDFs since it is found in Umbria only outside the Natura 2000 Network sites. For this group of vertebrates, 75% of the values of the population parameter indicate that the relationship between the size of the populations present in the Natura 2000 Network sites in Umbria and those present nationally is less than 2% (C) and in the remaining cases, the populations are considered insignificant (D). The degree of conservation of the habitat elements important for fish species is suboptimal in more than 55% of cases, while the populations would not seem to have a high level of isolation. Evaluating the general situation, the contribution of the sites to the conservation of the species is good or excellent in nearly 60% of cases. This fact, however, does not seem to be consistent with the real SC of the species in Umbria. Nationally, the last report on the conservation of species of European interest (ISPRA 194-2014) presented an inadequate or unfavourable SC in most cases; these data are also confirmed on the regional level, as emerges from the monitoring under the Umbria Fish Charter.

Amphibians. For this class of vertebrates, about 60% of the values of the population parameter indicate that the populations present in the Natura 2000 Network sites in Umbria are considered insignificant (D) and most of the remaining data highlight that the ratio between the size of the populations present in the Natura 2000 Network sites in Umbria and those present nationally is less than 2% (C). An analysis of the degree of conservation of the habitat elements important for amphibians in the sites shows that for about 60% of the values in the SDFs are missing an assessment, while the remaining 40% are distributed between a "good" (30%) and "average or limited" (10%, C) degree of conservation. The evaluation of the low degree of isolation of the species population, together with a mostly good SC of biological habitats, determines an overall assessment of the value of the sites for the conservation of the species between excellent (A) and good (B) for about 20% of the data. An absence of reference parameters emerges for about 60% of the values.

Reptiles. In most cases for this group of vertebrates, all the criteria to assess the SC of the sites for the species signalled in the SDFs highlight the absence of information useful for establishing possible degrees of significance. In fact, 95% of the values in the "population" parameter indicate that the ratio between the size of the populations of reptiles present in the Natura 2000 Network sites in Umbria and those present nationally is "insignificant". The parameters "degree of conservation of the biological habitat elements important for the species", "degree of isolation of the population" and "overall assessment" are indicated only for some species in some sites, highlighting the lack of information for most reptiles.

Birds. From analysis of the SDFs of the sites in the Natura 2000 Network in Umbria, the pygmy cormorant (Phalacrocorax pygmeus), the great egret (Casmerodius albus), and the calandra lark (Melanocorypha calandra) are not noted, although they are present in the territory. An examination of the information about the avifauna contained in the SDFs shows that an absence of indications about the evaluation criteria emerges for most species and in most sites (about 80% of the values). In cases where the population parameter is indicated, the values mainly report a ratio between the size of the populations of birds present in the Natura 2000 Network sites in Umbria and those present nationally of less than 2% (C), despite the overall emergence of a low degree of isolation (C). By observing the values indicated on the degree of conservation of the habitat elements that are biologically important for the species, it also emerges that in most cases, a "good" (B) or "excellent" (A) degree of conservation can be identified. For some species at least, this leads to an overall assessment of the contribution of the sites to the conservation of the species of "good" (B) or "excellent" (A).

Mammals. From analysis of the SDFs, the common barbastelle (Barbastella barbastellus) is not present in that it is detected only outside the Natura 2000 Network sites in Umbria, while the presence of the whiskered bat (Myotis mystacinus), the soprano pipistrelle (Pipistrellus pygmaeus), and the brown long-eared bat (Plecotus auritus) within the Natura 2000

Network is wrongly omitted. For this reason, updates are necessary, in particular in sites IT5210009, IT5210071, IT5220003, and IT5220023. Assessing the information about the mammals contained in the SDFs, a ratio between the size of the populations of mammals present in the Natura 2000 Network sites in Umbria and those present nationally of less than 2% (C) emerges for about 50% of the data and about 30% "insignificant". The presence of a consistent number of species with non-isolated populations, however, allows for an overall "good" (B) assessment of the value of the site for the conservation of some mammals.

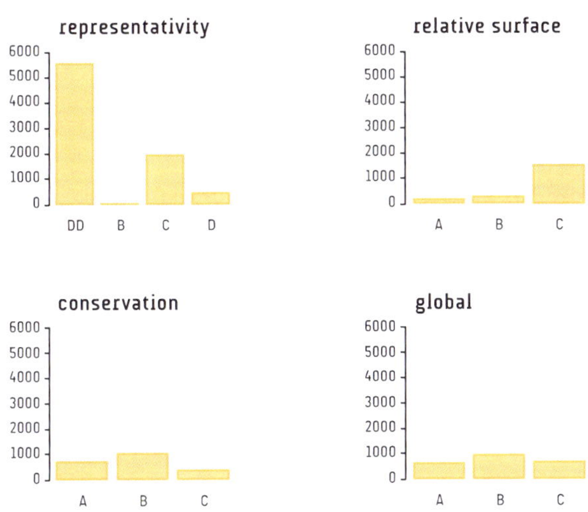

Fig.3 Graphical summary of frequency data for sites in Umbria for the categories of judgement for each assessment criterion used for the animal species in Annexes II, IV, and V HD and in Annex I BD in accordance with the Natura 2000 Network Standard Data Form (European Commission, 2011).

References

- Commissione Europea, 2011. Decisione di esecuzione della Commissione dell'11 luglio 2011 concernente un formulario informativo sui siti da inserire nella Rete Natura 2000 [notificata con il numero C (2011) 4892]. 2011/484/UE. ALLEGATO - Rete Natura 2000. FORMULARIO STANDARD. Gazzetta ufficiale dell'Unione europea, L198: 39-70.
- Ercole S., Giacanelli V., Bacchetta G., Fenu G., Genovesi P. (Eds.), 2016. Manuali per il monitoraggio di specie e habitat di interesse comunitario (Direttiva 92/43/CEE) in Italia: specie vegetali. ISPRA, Serie Manuali e linee guida, 140/2016.
- Gigante D., Alessandrini A., Ballelli S., Bartolucci F., Conti F., Ferri V., Gubellini L., Hofmann N., Montagnani C., Pinzi M., Venanzoni R., Wagensommer R.P.., 2014. *Klasea lycopifolia* (Vill.) Á. Löve et D. Löve. Inf. Bot. Ital., 46(1): 128-131. ISSN: 0020-0697

Analysis and assessment of the means of managing the Natura 2000 Network sites in Umbria

City planning

Alessandro Marucci, Francesco Zullo, Lorena Fiorini, Bernardino Romano

DICEAA, University of L'Aquila

A recognition of the existing plans in cities in the Umbria Region was made in order to create a mosaic of them on the regional level. The aim was to build a well-structured GIS database and to draft a technical protocol for the Region that would allow synchronous dialogue

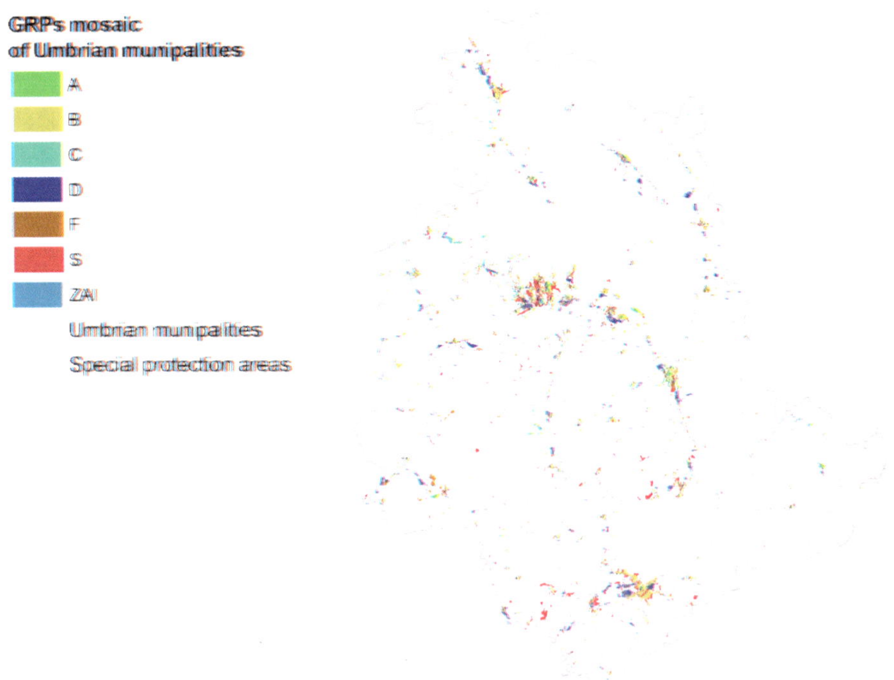

Fig.1 The complete mosaic of the general regulatory plans deriving from the ADP and SUN LIFE projects.

between the planning tools and existing plans at any level of operation.
For the procedure adopted, reference is made to the document to update the parks in Umbria (ADP- http://www.parcodelnera.it/piani-di-gestione-dei-parchi-dellumbria/), in which the same working group (UNIVAQ) developed the mosaic of 32 General Regulatory Plans (GRP). Within the SUN LIFE project, data related to the GRPs of the remaining 60 municipalities in Umbria were processed, thereby completing the mosaic for the entire Region (Figure 1).

The framework of land planning

The completion of the mosaic of the GRPs highlighted a rather diversified situation (Graphs 1–2, Figure 2). Although the majority of municipalities have latest-generation plans following LR 11/2005, there is a decent presence of building programmes (about 16.5%), dating to the 1970s and 1990s (albeit with some updates).

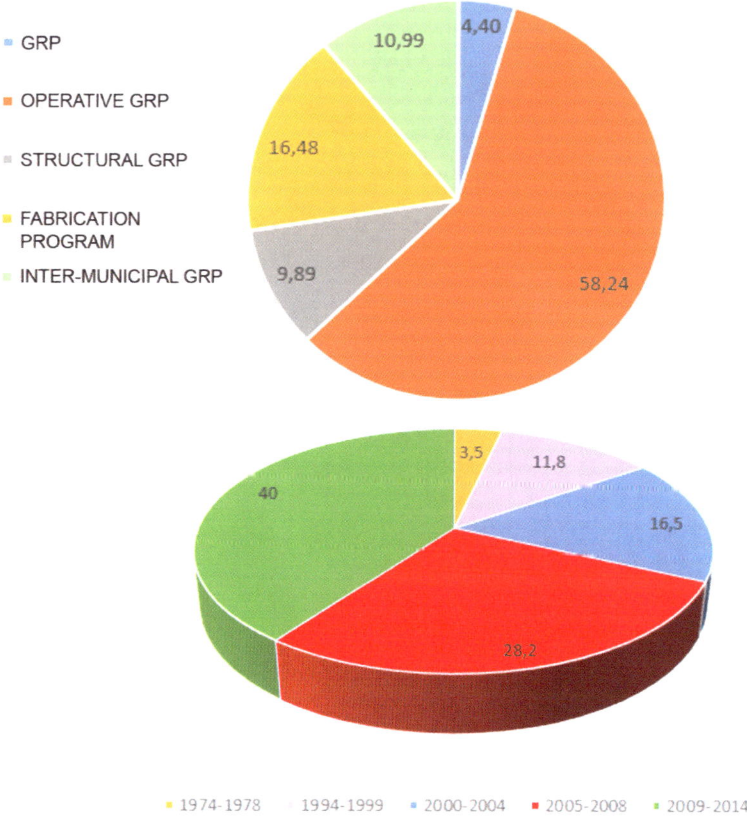

Graf.1- 2 Above, the percentage of types of GRP currently present in Umbria. Below, the percentage of plans in operation when they were drafted.

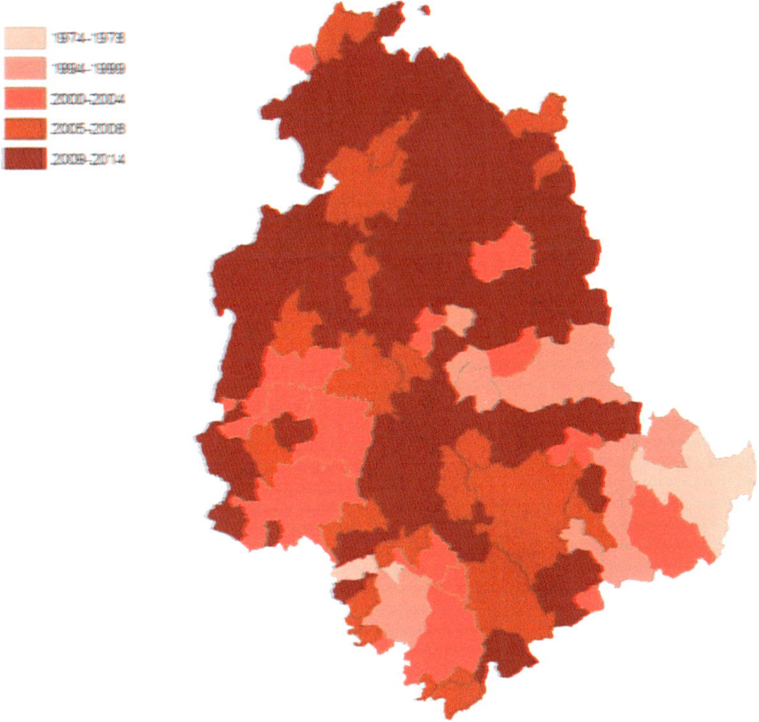

Fig.2 Map showing the geographical distribution of the GRPs (or latest modification) by length of time in force.

Many GRPs were developed (or modified) following the identification of the sites of European importance, but the presence of settlement provisions within them, while limited, confirms the difficulty of integrating environmental aspects in ordinary territorial planning, especially on the local scale.

The overall data regarding the content of the GRPs depict the following:

- about 2,000 ha of A zones, with historical characteristics;
- nearly 10,000 ha of B zones, in different stages of urbanization and construction where there are usually actions to complete the fabric;
- nearly 4,000 ha of C zones (residential), which regard areas of settlement expansion;
- slightly less than 7,500 ha of D zones (productive);
- in the service sector, there are about 2,000 ha for general facilities and more than 7,000 ha of spaces for collective use.

An initial verification showed that nearly half of the possible expansion of C, D, F, and S is still expressed. That is, it is present in the planning designs, but still has not been activated. This would imply that more than 10,000 ha of territory can still be urbanized in a time frame that reasonably extends over the next 5–10 years.

The goal of this work was to obtain quantitative information regarding the relationship between the SACs and urban-panning provisions in the municipal GRPs. The analysis, made through geoprocessing techniques and statistical calculations, resulted in a relatively detailed framework of reciprocal interference from which current and potential critical elements emerged clearly.

Note that for the mosaic of existing GRPs, after appropriately aligning the synoptic frameworks, only the parts subject to settlement projects (uniform zones A, B, C, D, F, and services) were considered, using the same method as for the ADP.

The GRP mosaic allowed the urban-planning provisions expressed in the plans to be analysed through zoning in relation to the parameters of the SAC from both a quantitative

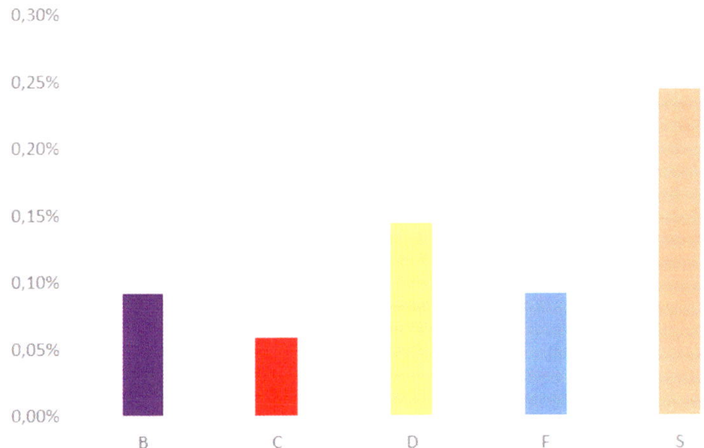

Graf.3 Percentage distribution (y-axis) of GRP provisions (x-axis) in the regional system of Natura 2000 Network sites.

(Figures 3 and 4) and qualitative point of view.

Overall, the presence of settlement expansion in the Natura 2000 Network is rather low, with the percentages indicated in Graph 3.

As well, the new expansions affect 0.23% of the habitat surface area, but are more often located next to or a few metres away. The distribution of land-planning provisions within the habitats is prevalent in the zones destined for services, which cover more than half of the surface area of interference, followed by zones to complete residential and productive areas. Very low interference is seen between the settlement provisions of the urban-planning tools and within the Natura 2000 Network areas, while the situation is rather different outside of it.

SAC DENOMINATION	Urbanized area established in existing GRPs
Monte la Pelosa - Colle Fergiara (Nera Valley)	2,03
Mineral water springs (Parrano)	2,17
Tiber River between San Giustino and Pierantonio	2,28
Forests and moors of Panicarola	2,51
Vetorno Creek	3,16
Topino River (Bagnara - Nocera Umbra)	3,41
Roccaporena - Monte della Sassa	3,65
Monte Torre Maggiore (Martani Mountains)	4,27
Forests of Monti di Sodolungo - Rosso (Città di Castello)	4,76
Campiano Valley (Preci)	6,09
Pettino Valley (Campello sul Clitunno)	7,39
Lake Alviano	7,63
Monte Cucco (peak)	7,69
Ruschio plains (Stroncone)	8,96
Forests and meadows of Fratticiola Selvatica (Valfabbrica)	10,34
Forests of Farneta (Monte Castrilli)	10,44
Lake Corbara	11,48
Nera Valley	11,62
Forests of Ferretto - Bagnolo	11,98
Lake Piediluco - Monte Caperno	13,57
Martani foothills (Bettona - Gualdo Cattaneo)	18,12
Forests of the high Nestore Valley	21,72
Lake San Liberato	26,35
Monti Maggio - Nero (peak)	27,58
Monte Malbe	43,79
Lake Trasimeno	112,56
Sibillini Mountains (slopes in Umbria)	198,15
TOTAL	528,98

Fig.3 Distribution of surface area that can potentially be urbanized as indicated by the GRPs in the SACs for the single sites.

In particular, the analysis revealed the following critical points:
- Provision of productive settlements within the Natura 2000 Network sites. The presence of some production centres within the Natura 2000 Network sites represents an element that could potentially alter their ecosystem functionality. The analysis showed that the situations with the greatest interference are located in the SAC of Lake Trasimeno, where

the future settlements would be located next to habitat 3150, Mount La Pelosa, the Nera valley, and the Campiano valley in habitat 9210, and the Martani Mountains within habitat 9340.

- Provision of residential expansions (B and C) within Natura 2000 Network sites. Numerically, these are more important sites that affect 0.18% of the SAC and 0.05% of habitats. In

Municipality	GRP surface area in N2000 sites (ha)
Alviano	2,96
Avigliano Umbro	10,44
Baschi	13,48
Bettona	20,12
Campello sul Clitunno	7,39
Cascia	3,65
Castiglion del Lago	66,49
Cerreto di Spoleto	6,49
Città di Castello	2,28
Fosato di Vico	3,16
Gualdo Tadino	27,58
Guardea	4,67
Magione	4,05
Narni	26,35
Nocera Umbra	3,41
Norcia	124,47
Panicale	2,51
Parrano	2,17
Passignano sul trasimeno	28,37
Perugio	43,79
Piegaro	27,72
Polino	2,03
Preci	22,28
Sigillo	7,69
Stroncone	8,96
Terni	17,85
Tuoro sul Trasimeno	28,29
Valfabrica	10,34
TOTAL	**528,98**

Fig.4 Distribution of surface area that can potentially be urbanized as indicated by the GRPs in the SACs for the single municipalities.

most cases, this relates to provisions regarding inhabited centres affected by waterways included in the SAC, such as the Vetorno Creek (in the centre of Fossato di Vico), where the plan locates service areas interfering with habitat 92A0, and zones of expansion and completion in close proximity. An analogous situation is seen in the Valnerina SAC in the municipality of Ferentillo, where settlements and services have been planned along the Nera River.

As already mentioned above, a rather different condition regards the territorial matrix of Natura 2000 Network sites where provisions to increase urbanized areas are much more conspicuous and widespread and risk ecologically besieging and suffocating the Natura 2000 Network areas. The result would be the obstruction of permeability towards the exterior and towards other sectors suitable for guaranteeing biotic fluxes that are essential to conserving biodiversity.

Planning on the supralocal scale

Massimo Sargolini, Paolo Perna, Andrea Renzi

SAAD School of Architecture and Design – UNICAM University of Camerino

Natura 2000 Network sites surely represents an important step forward in the evolution of the concept of nature protection, positioned as a new tool to accompany the traditional organization of protection through parks and reserves. It is a complex system of ecologically interconnected areas that overlap not only with themselves and with areas protected under Law 394/91, but also with intensely anthropized areas. The Habitats Directive 92/43/EEC, which instituted the Natura 2000 Network, presents some innovative characteristics and absolute value for its approach to biodiversity conservation. For the scope of this work, at least three aspects will be underlined.

The first regards the identification of areas important for conserving the habitats and species of European interest, which constitute the Natura 2000 Network. While these are central for its application, the coherence of the network is guaranteed "through [national] land-use planning and development [policies]" (Art. 10). This takes the objective of biodiversity protection to all sectors of territorial government that could potentially contribute, thereby going well beyond simple assessment of the lack of negative effects.

The second regards the fields of interest in the Directive. It does not establish regulatory measures a priori, i.e., valid as soon as the sites are identified, but "simply" asks that their state of conservation is guaranteed to be satisfactory, adopting the local measures necessary and only when existing regulations are not sufficient. It is clear that the centrality of conservation is therefore preferentially charged with the "ordinary management" of the territory.

The third regards the list of habitats and species of European interest, whose conservation should be guaranteed. Many are tied to traditional human activities that therefore play a positive role in conserving biodiversity.

From this consideration, it is clear how the application of the Directive is closely tied to an overall adaptation of territorial and sector policies that should not only not contrast with, but be an essential tool in activating the network.

For this reason, and in order to define regional policies for activating the Natura 2000 Network, it is essential to understand how the plans and programs relate to it, both in terms of the territories and sectors under the various government entities.

The Umbria Region was among the first Italian Regions to adopt site-specific conservation measures, which represented the starting point for this work. In fact, with them, it was possible to define the overall framework of necessary actions to guarantee the conservation of the network. For this scope, all the plans were analysed in detail, and a database was created to synthesize the various measures, organizing them into three main categories: prohibitions, actions to incentivize, and actions to incentivize in particular habitats.

In this way, it was possible to create a synthetic list, overcoming minimal differences in the wording of the regulations or modifications tied to the different habitats present in the sites. At the end of this phase, 59 prohibitions, 153 actions to incentivize, and 96 actions to incentivize in particular habitats were identified.

There was a clear need at this point to classify the measures according to environment, which would allow the existing relationships between the Natura 2000 Network regulations and the planning of the different territorial entities to be compared clearly and objectively. Consistent with the management of the Natura 2000 Network, functional groups were used, which we defined as areas of interference based on the second hierarchical level of list of pressures, threats, and actions, made available by the EU to compile the Standard Data Forms for the sites. Each measure was assigned to one or more areas defined such that it would be clear which category of pressure/threat it responded to.

In the second phase, the supralocal plans were analysed, regarding in particular all the plans on the regional and provincial scale for landscape/environmental protection (TUP, PPR, PTCP), territorial development (TUP, Strategic Territorial Design, etc.), and the organization and delineation of the limits and protections in the entire regional territory. Further investigations were made into sector plans that provide regulatory, obligatory, incentivizing, or strategic indications on circumscribed thematic areas, but which often directly affect Natura 2000 Network sites. Among the latter, the following can be named: the Water Protection Plan, the Hydrogeological Structure Plan, the Waste Management Plan, the Energy Plan, as well as others. For each plan, beyond a general characterization, which evaluated in particular if and how the Natura 2000 Network entered into their definition, a detailed analysis was made of their organization, assigning each individual provision to one or more of the areas of interference mentioned above.

The third and last phase consisted in a comparison of the conservation measures and provisions of the plans and programmes regarding the same areas of interference. This permitted an assessment of whether the plans and programmes interfere with the conservation measures and if so, whether the interference translates as a criticality, a partial criticality or lack due to the generic nature of the regulations or, finally, if it acts in synergy with the conservation measures.

Based on the above-mentioned evaluations, a final comment could be formulated for each plan that highlighted how they could be acted upon to make them functional in activating the Natura 2000 Network in the forms designated by the Region.

In some cases, the study of the various planning tools highlighted "coherence" problems between the conservation measures established in the management plan and the indications foreseen by ordinary planning. More in general, the fragmentation or even total absence of specific indications seems to emerge regarding Natura 2000 Network sites within the different forms and types of planning. While the Umbria Region has an organized, updated regulatory and planning system, the incidence of Natura 2000 Network sites is often relegated to minimal regulatory references or simple references to a specific regulation. While this aspect also descends from the higher level of Natura 2000 Network planning with respect to other forms of territorial government, it is also possible that the relative "youth" of this level of planning still has not allowed some areas of planning to be updated to include specific proactive provisions in the planning of these portions of territory.

The Natura 2000 Network and ecosystem services

Lucia Rocchi, Carla Cortina, Luisa Paolotti, Antonio Boggia

DSA3, University of Perugia

Ecosystem services (ES) were traditionally protected by the Umbria Region with regulatory tools, but the recent trend has been for an approach that is more aware of economic tools, including market ones.

The Italian government is currently authorized to adopt one or more legislative decrees to introduce a payment system for ESs and the environment (PSEA), as prescribed by Art. 70 of the so-called "Environmental Connection" (Ddl 1676-A). The PSEA system will be activated especially in the presence of public intervention to assign property rights or the use of a natural good of common interest. In particular, it is expected that when defining the PSEA system, the services to be paid, their value, and the related contractual obligations and means of payment are specifically identified.

The Natura 2000 Network, as a key element in the green infrastructure (EU, 2013) – that is, the multifunctional network of green spaces, both new and existing, both rural and urban, in support of natural and ecological processes, a fundamental component for the health and quality of life of the communities – should also:

- reinforce the functionality of the ecosystems, increasing their resilience in order to constantly provide goods and services;
- stem the loss of biodiversity, increasing connectivity between existing natural areas and improving the permeability of the landscape;
- mitigate the effects of climate change and improve the quality of life of humans (in the fields of health, tourism, green-economy opportunities, and conservation of the historical and cultural heritage).

Investments in management measures and the strong legal protection applied to the network can increase the range of services provided and guarantee their flow in the long term.

The assessment of the ESs provided by large categories of habitats made in the SUN LIFE project highlighted that the ESs in Umbria consist of support services and services to provide essential goods and regulate ecosystem and cultural processes supplied by grouping habitats that have ecologically similar characteristics.

The economic assessment of services supplied by the habitats in the Natura 2000 Network in Umbria:

- serve as support in allocating resources among programmes to conserve biodiversity and other initiatives of social interest;
- contribute to the design of economic incentives and institutional agreements;

- justify the budges destined to conserving biodiversity;
- define the priorities in the conservation programmes.

The estimates made through the choice experiment method led to an evaluation of the overall willingness of the population in Umbria to pay for two levels of protection, for each large category of habitat identified. Similar values were found for different habitats since it is possible that they provide similar ESs. These are annual values and refer to a five-year commitment. According to the two hypothetical levels of protection, the values oscillated between about €10 million and €16 million for the zoned habitats and for some of the non-zoned habitats (grassy and marshy river habitats, shrubbed river habitats, and swampy forested river habitats) and between €8 million and €13.5 million for other zoned habitats. For the habitats outside zones, a single result equal to about €3 million was found, independent of the level of protection.

Beyond supporting the allocation of resources among biodiversity-conservation programmes and other initiatives of social interest, justifying the budgets destined for biodiversity conservation, and helping to define priorities in conservation programmes, the economic assessment of the ESs supplied by the Natura 2000 Network in Umbria can also contribute to establishing the network management strategies that would be best accepted by local populations.

In Umbria, based on the results obtained from the research, considering the various scenarios hypothesized in the analysis and the aggregation into large habitats, the annual return in terms of ecosystem services ranges from €89,835,748 to €137,858,040.

With regard to management costs, it is estimated that in the past period of European funding (2007–2013), annual spending for the Natura 2000 Network was €7,467,000/year (considering the initial effective period of spending and its extension after expiration, the time period for these costs is in reality 2008–2015).

The estimate of annual management costs of the Natura 2000 Network in Umbria for current programming (and even beyond, given that the period considered is 2017–2023) instead amounts to €11,180,000/year.

Therefore, in Umbria as in the EU, the costs sustained by society in the past and those to be sustained in the coming years have served and will serve to conserve a value that is anyway very high for society itself. This is in itself a great indicator of the efficiency and effectiveness of spending, and provides security and guarantees to public decision-makers regarding the worth, at least on the financial plane, of what is established in the planning document to manage the Natura 2000 Network.

The Natura 2000 Network and green jobs

Marco Gisotti, Oliviero Spinelli

Comunità Ambiente

Due to their nature, green jobs represent a transverse change in production cycles and/or services.

In fact, these are not simply new professions, but a reinvention or adaptation of existing professions towards green skills and knowledge. For example, the fact that among the soft skills requested throughout the working world, the propensity for sustainability and energy efficiency now exceeds digital skills (Unioncamere, Indagine Excelsior 2018, in preparation), demonstrates the pervasiveness of this trend not only in terms of concrete application, but also in terms of progressive cultural adaptation of production and service-based processes. The system of businesses registered in 2012 in the territory of the Natura 2000 Network in Umbria include 1,529 companies with an entrepreneurial density of 12.1 units per 100 residents. The activity sectors are mostly represented by agricultural companies (23.5%), commerce (20%), and activities tied to tourism and provision (10.0%). With regard to artisan companies and provision, this stands at 25.6%, higher than the value of Natura 2000 Network areas in central Italy (25%) by about 0.6%, and by 2.7% if the equivalent national value of the network is used (22.9%). Data related to agricultural activities are also very significant. These represent the dominant economic sector, with 23.5% of all businesses committed to these activities and a percentage of 60.6% of agricultural surface area in use with respect to the total (data from 2010). This value is significantly above the value for central Italy (18.9%) and the nation (18.1%) with respect to the Natura 2000 Network areas (Ministry of the Environment and Protection of Land and Sea and Unioncamere, 2014. L'economia reale nei Parchi nazionali e nelle aree naturali protette).

These numbers therefore represent a particularly active socioeconomic fabric which entails not only supporting educational and orientation activities in themselves, but promoting a policy that favours the evolution of a cultural environment that is favourable to a more effective transition to green jobs.

The most recent job-market survey in Natura 2000 Network areas in Umbria (Ibid.) shows that the number of skilled workers in the Region from 1991–2011 has increased by 4.7%, counter to the national trend in Natura 2000 Network areas, which has instead registered a decrease of 1.9%. The possibility of drawing advantages in terms of management and enhancement of the Natura 2000 Network is therefore not limited to just the professions closely involved in activities to manage the areas themselves, but tend to expand to the different activities that have developed in the territory, whether they are production- or service-based, for management or research.

An important aspect of green jobs is the transverse nature of the skills. In fact, multi- and trans-disciplinary activities are frequent. For example, multi-functional agricultural companies also lend themselves to agritourism. Here, agriculture, environmental teaching, accommodation, and oenogastronomy come together seamlessly, requiring that each individual figure, which could traditionally be identified with a specific professional unit, instead acquires skills for other ends, such that the figure could even substitute some steps in the production chain.

While companies that need new or renewed figures are emerging, the role of research and area management is not undervalued, for which public entities and associations need more specific profiles that are not only technical/scientific, as would reasonably be expected, but also capable of interacting with the territory as environmental educators and communicators.

The investigation made in the SUN LIFE project highlights how the system of protected and/or Natura 2000 Network areas offers important opportunities for the near future in some key areas. Ecotourism, or environmental tourism without a shared definition in the literature, is one of these, creating green ways, enhancing and pertaining to the so-called "wildlife economy". In the same way, new forms of agriculture that are increasingly multi-functional can be flywheels of businesses that are not only more respectful of the territory but also more efficient. In the commerce sector, this includes an energy policy oriented around efficiency, the use of renewables and smart grids, circular economic growth, and the transformation of the waste sector in a virtuous chain of recovery and reuse of post-consumer products.

As it emerges from the study, all of this will be possible especially thanks to interventions for greater coordination and orientation by the institutions, also regenerating the educational sector with a push towards new models of green jobs increasingly tied to the analysis of professional needs in Umbria.

3

PROJECT OUTPUT

3.1

Management strategy

Livia Bellisari, Oliviero Spinelli

Comunità Ambiente

The management strategy for the Natura 2000 Network in Umbria was produced under the SUN LIFE project. It aims to protect, conserve, and restore the functioning of the natural systems and halt the loss of biodiversity in Umbria.

The drafting was entrusted to a group of interdisciplinary experts in: planning and management of Natura 2000 Network sites, habitats, and species, monitoring, conservation measures, regional policies, legal/administrative matters, communication, agriculture, economics, green jobs, territorial marketing, climate change, water management, and the landscape.

In addition to specific analyses and assessments, identification of the objectives was based on preliminary studies made in the initial phases of the SUN LIFE project, such as assessment of the state of conservation of the habitats and species, the planning and regulatory framework of reference, the available financial resources, the employment perspectives, an estimate of the value of ecosystem services, and the communication plan.

Based on the specific skills and strategic needs already identified by the Umbria Region when drafting the project proposal, the working group defined a series of objectives that come together to maintain and improve the state of conservation of the regional Natura 2000 Network.

The management strategy thus developed was subjected to comparison both within the region (through the Natura 2000 Network Group) and through territorial meetings that saw the participation of the main stakeholders on a regional level.

The strategy therefore represents the general guidance tool aimed at achieving the Umbria Region's effective management of the Natura 2000 Network. This is not a formal planning tool and therefore should not be formally adopted. The strategy does not have limited validity, but is monitored and possibly updated periodically.

The objectives and actions identified were assigned a priority related to preparation or urgency and the priorities were defined through a specific document, the PAF (Prioritized Action Framework). The specific management measures will then be identified or updated under the appropriate tools, such as the management plans for the individual Natura 2000 Network sites.

The strategy is organized into a general part with an introduction to the context and method and a middle part in which the objectives are defined along with the monitoring method and some attachments.

The introductory parts frame the strategy within the context of the Natura 2000 Network and the regulatory and governance framework; the methodology defines the framework of application and management. The definition of the objectives and the related actions represents the heart of the document in its strategic and orientation function. The monitoring defines the method of verification and updating. The attachments mainly include preliminary analysis documents developed under the SUN LIFE project that contributed to the definition of the objectives.

The strategy is composed of eight large objectives:

1. Optimization of the management of the regional network.
2. Management and conservation of the habitats in Annex I of the Habitats Directive.
3. Management and conservation of the species in Annexes II, IV, and V of the Habitats Directive and Annex I of the Birds Directive.
4. Management of alien species.
5. Revision of municipal urban-planning tools for the conservation, expansion, and restoration of ecological connectivity between habitat patches.
6. Management, conservation, and regeneration of the landscape in its relationships with biodiversity.
7. Promoting green jobs tied to the Natura 2000 Network.
8. Improving awareness and information about the value of the Natura 2000 Network areas and their ecosystem services.

Each large objective was therefore refined into specific objectives and actions that ought to be implemented to reach the general objective: the effective management of the Network. For each action, the habitats and/or species and/or sites referred to by the action were identified. For each objective, the entities responsible and main sources of financing were defined. A specific financial plan was also produced to identify the available resources that can be activated.

Optimizing the management of the regional network

Maria Grazia Possenti

Umbria Region

The objective set by the Umbria Region was to improve the management capacity of the regional network through the creation of a management structure that would guarantee the effectiveness of the conservation actions, economic sustainability and techniques, and increase the skills of the people involved. This result could be reached by intensifying cooperation between the regional authorities in charge of the Natura 2000 Network at the various levels, even harmonizing the procedures and simplifying the VINCA. To this end, it was deemed necessary to create a negotiating table for regional territorial managers to define criteria for consistency when issuing opinions about interventions that interfere with Natura 2000 Network sites.

It will also be important to train personnel from the public entities and professional associations in order to increase their competences regarding the Natura 2000 Network (management of habitats and species) and also the planning capacity by organizing training courses, seminars, workshops, and conferences.

Another important point for reaching the objective is coordination with surrounding Regions to manage bordering sites in order to share coordinated procedures and implement a process to harmonize the application of the assessment of environmental incidence.

As well, in consideration of the fact that the Umbria Region has all the management plans for the Natura 2000 Network sites within the territory, these will be reviewed and updated by activating sub-measure 7.1 in the 2014–2020 RDP.

Since the territorial areas concerning the Natura 2000 Network in Umbria largely fall on private property in which productive and economic activities are necessarily included, it is necessary to promote forms of management that are coordinated between the public and private spheres by providing guidelines and general criteria to stipulate agreements aimed at managing these areas.

What is absolutely necessary is the harmonization and integration of the regulation on the Natura 2000 Network in Umbria with other European, national, and regional regulations. In fact, the preparatory analysis made under the SUN LIFE project, highlighted the need to define paths aimed at overcoming the critical points regarding the regional regulatory framework, identifying possible solutions and spokespeople. In addition, it will be necessary to propose modifications to and/or integrations for the regulations that present specific criticalities.

Finally, a part of the Monte Sibillini National Park and seven regional parks fall within the regional territory. The planning of protected natural areas identified with Law 394/91 will therefore be harmonized with the Natura 2000 Network sites falling within them by recognizing conservation measures in the park plans and the cartographic identification of community habitats in the areas affected by the parks.

Objectives 2, 3 and 4

Management and conservation of the Habitats in Annex I of the HD in Annexes II, IV, and V of the HD and Annex I of the BD – Management of alien invasive species

Daniela Gigante, Fabio Maneli, Roberto Venanzoni, Laura Pompei, Massimo Lorenzoni

DCBB, University of Perugia

Cristiano Spilinga, Francesca Montioni, Silvia Carletti, Emi Petruzzi

Studio Naturalistico Hyla

From the botanical and zoological points of view, the strategy was built starting from the various products developed under the SUN LIFE project. The "Diagnostic manual of Habitats and species in Umbria", available online, represents a tool of fundamental importance to diagnose, recognize, and update knowledge about Habitats and species in the Natura 2000 Network in Umbria. This is a point of reference for multiple objectives in the strategy and it is necessary for identifying transformation trends in light of the monitoring results (former Art. 17). The development of specific monitoring guidelines for plant and animal species and habitats resulted in simple but effective procedures to collect balanced data based on shared principles and standardized techniques; the guidelines are useful for providing comparable information on the local, regional, and national scales. With regard to each plant species and habitat, a sheet containing methodological indications on the monitoring techniques was provided. The approach for large areas, based on dividing the regional territory into uniform areas (wet zones, plain-hill landscape, Apennine landscape) allowed the parameters considered to be better quantified to assess the state of conservation of the species and habitats.

The protocols developed refer to more consolidated scientific methods in the fields of plant science and species monitoring, populations, and plant and animal communities and habitats, and consider the indications contained in the National Manuals produced by ISPRA (Ercole et al., 2016; Angelini et al., 2016; Stoch & Genovesi, 2016). The standardized protocols were integrated based on the characteristics of the Natura 2000 Network in Umbria, in consideration of local criticalities, intrinsic characteristics, and the regional distribution characteristics of the 41 Habitats in Annex I, the 8 (plus one extinct) plant species, the 82 animal species in Annexes II, IV, and V Habitats Directive, and the 50 bird species in Annex I Habitats Directive; these were also weighted with reference to the general national and European framework. The process to prioritize the species and Habitats also allowed the monitoring and management priorities to be defined, thereby entering into the assessment of the appropriate methods and time frames to apply the various protocols and providing the strategy with a solid key to choose the priority measures to insert in the PAF.

The SUN LIFE project also developed a protocol to collect germplasms of the plant species in Annexes II, IV, and V present in Umbria, creating for each a sheet containing practical information (type of seeds, condition of conservation, germination, and identification of possible regional "donor areas"). This tool constitutes valid support for those measures in the PAF dedicated to Habitat restoring/strengthening or reinforcing populations of plant species.

In formulating a strategy coherent with the conservation needs of the Natura 2000 Network in Umbria, particular importance was placed on the management of alien invasive species (AIS), one of the main criticalities on the regional level that emerged over the course of the SUN LIFE project. AISs, in fact, threaten the survival of indigenous species; they can compromise the integrity of the Habitats and in many cases cause serious damage to production activities and can even threaten human health.

The strategy proposed therefore foresees the development of management policies based on a hierarchical approach that prioritizes the prevention of new introductions, early detection, and the development of surveillance models. The actions formulated within the strategy aim to reduce the number of alien species present in the regional territory by adopting measures for long-term control and containment and the mitigation of negative effects produced on the structure and function of the biocenoses.

In addition, the strategy underlines the importance of developing good practices and raising awareness about the problem among citizens (citizen science) and workers in the field.

Revision of city-level urban-planning tools for conservation, expansion, recovery of ecological connectivity between patches of habitat

Alessandro Marucci, Francesco Zullo, Lorena Fiorini, Bernardino Romano

DICEAA, University of L'Aquila

The expected result relates to the monitoring and increase in efficiency of local planning with the goal of maintaining the environmental continuity of the matrix. Reaching this large objective assumes an initial phase of ordinary recognition of the content of municipal urban-planning tools. To this end, these tools were analysed in order to assess the settlement pressure on Natura 2000 Network sites and provide the procedures necessary to evaluate the potential effects of isolating these sites.

The motive justifying this method is the fact that, particular to Italy, municipal regulatory plans represent an important level on which decisions are made that influence the future of territorial transformations and as a consequence, the configuration of the overall ecological connectivity.

The results of this demanding recognition can be summarized in the following points:

* Assessment of the effects of the local planning system on environmental connectivity and of Natura 2000 Network sites in particular;
* Verification of the real impacts of urban plans on the Umbria Region Ecological Network (UREN);
* Identification of the potential for ecological connection among Natura 2000 Network sites: the effective ecological network (UREEN);
* Adaptation of the prescriptive configuration to maintain/improve the potential connectivity.

Implementation of the proposed actions produces an informational layer with varied utility for the Region, and the technical means of equipping this mosaic may be diverse, closely depending on the usable resources and objectives that are proposed. These can be summarized as follows:

a. monitoring of modifications to urban parts of the territory, guided by the plans. In this case, only those destinations inherent to the artificialization/construction/infrastructure building of the territory will be extracted to obtain scenarios for the dynamic structure of building expansion, public services, distribution and mobility networks, and related accessory functions;

b. complete monitoring of city planning, including all the uses contained in the urban-planning tools, including those not specifically related to urban-planning, such as limits and agricultural zones. In this case, the platform to be designed will entail the regulated coordination of municipalities' techniques to produce the plans, introducing processes for uniform output that will allow new plans (or modifications) to be inserted directly in the regional mosaic, avoiding complex semantic and regulatory interpretation by the regional offices, which can be rather subjective and exposed to numerous errors.

Objective 6

Management, conservation, and regeneration of the landscape in its relationships with biodiversity

Massimo Sargolini, Paolo Perna, Andrea Renzi

SAAD School of Architecture and Design – UNICAM University of Camerino

The objective is to act through the landscape and identify those essential actions with landscape importance to maintain and increase biodiversity. In this sense, the strategic line was organized by dividing Umbria into landscape areas based on the functional grouping of "Regional Landscapes" defined by the RLP. The landscape areas were defined using their dominant characteristics, which can be traced to three main types: the historical/cultural, physical/natural, and social/symbolic matrices. The dominant aspects determine a specific territorial image associated with the morphological and geographical characterization of the territory. The landscape areas were then characterized through proposed objectives that aim to conserve the landscape through some protection activities, as in the case of human practices (agriculture, forestry, shepherding) that can significantly influence the levels of biodiversity in the territory. Objectives were then proposed that foresee different management practices (incentives for shepherding, production-chain agreements, and agricultural/environmental agreements) for the components that characterize the quality landscape in Umbria in order to strengthen the values in play. Finally, the overall strategy can also encompass objectives that foresee the active regeneration of areas and landscape components, for example, improving the relationship between settlements and surrounding areas with high environmental value, especially in those areas where the social and human component is prevalent. The landscape areas identified are reported below.

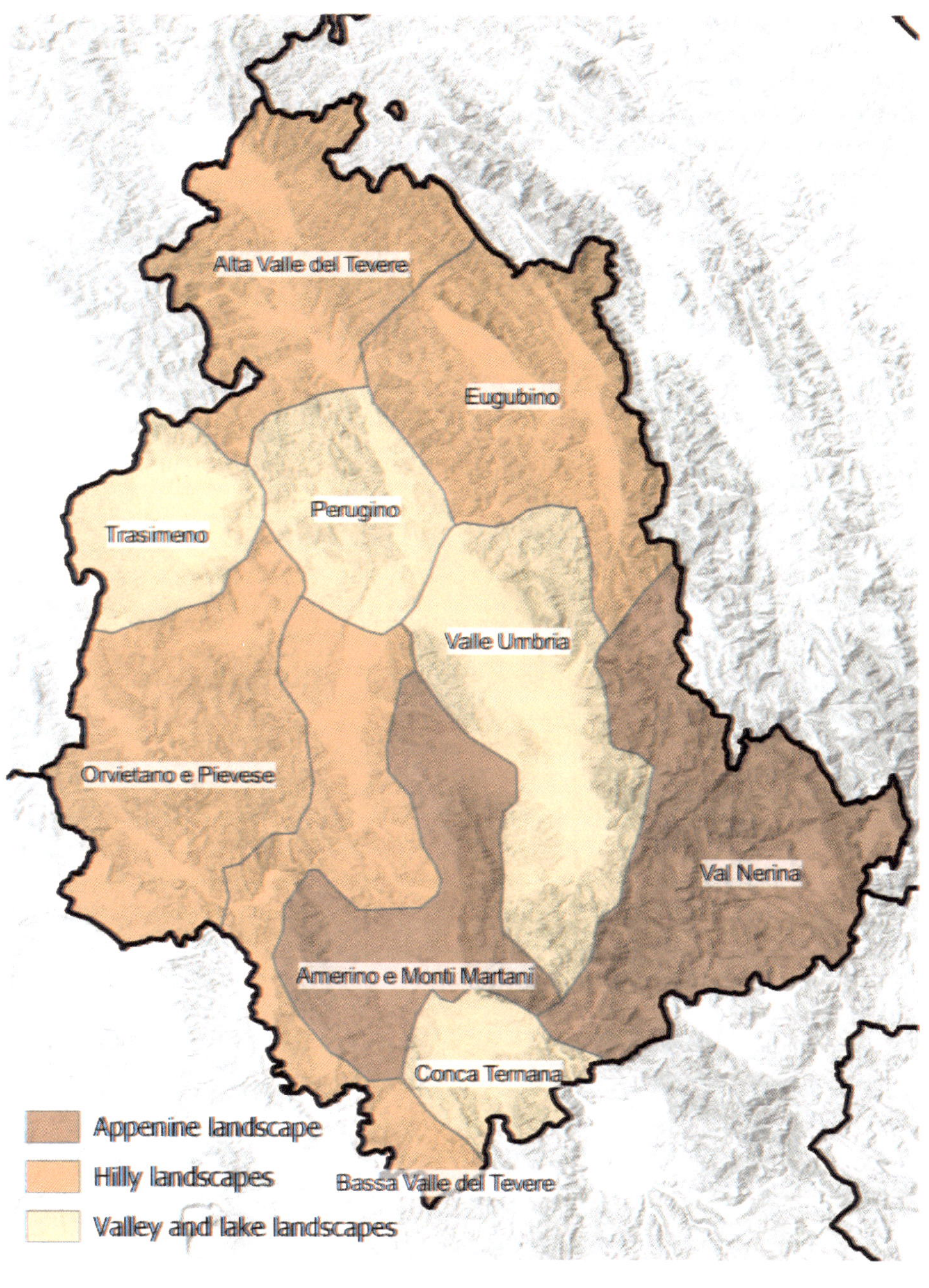

Fig.1 Landscape areas of Umbria Region

Apennine landscapes

The Apennine landscapes are distinguished as characteristic areas where the highest level of environmental resources is concentrated and where there is a significant degree of biodiversity. The objectives for this landscape area aim to protect and conserve the intrinsic characteristics of mountain areas, with special reference to the protection of biodiversity in Natura 2000 Network sites. In addition, some actions to reinforce and support agronomic and forestry/shepherding practices are proposed that imply a sustainable impact on the territory and the environment. The goal is to maintain a good level of landscape diversity and characterization, avoiding locally present phenomena and homogenization of components of the mountain landscape. In this area, the role played by water (as a resource) is very important. This is one of the axes supporting ecological connectivity and it can be managed and preserved by creating agreements or contracts between public and private subjects.

- *Apennine landscape with physical/natural characteristics and historical/cultural elements spread throughout the Valnerina*
- *Apennine landscape with physical/natural characteristics in the Martani and Amerino Mountains*

Hilly landscapes

The rural hilly landscape in Umbria corresponds to the best-known territorial area, even outside the regional borders, with alternating and intertwining natural/environmental components (morphological structure of the territory, presence of forested patches and waterways), components tied to traditional agricultural uses on the hillsides (olive trees and vineyard landscapes), and finally anthropic components of exceptional value, for example, the numerous historical hilltop towns that enrich the framework of the landscape characteristics present. In addition protecting the quality and numerous values present, the actions in this area aim to emphasize the reinforcement and enhancement of prestigious elements, both natural elements – thus closely tied to the theme of biodiversity – and anthropic elements – therefore tied to maintaining traditional agricultural practices and enhancing the connections with the hillside towns.

- *High hill – sub-Apennine landscape with physical/natural characteristics and historical/cultural elements spread throughout the high Tiber Valley*
- *High hill landscape of Gubbio with historical/cultural characteristics*
- *Hilly landscape of Orvieto with historical/cultural characteristics*
- *Hilly landscape with physical/natural characteristics in the low Tiber Valley*

Valley and lake landscapes

The river valley and lake landscape are the most-used areas, characterized by human action where the ecological connections and values of biodiversity are threatened the most by urban expansion, settlement dispersion, and the capillary nature of the infrastructure system. In these areas, in order to guarantee both an increase in biodiversity and improve the landscape value, a series of actions are proposed to stitch together a new fabric of relationships between rural areas and the peri-urban areas of the settlements. The attempt that the strategy can implement regards the possibility that some portions of natural or

	Id	Strategic actions	Apennine landscapes		
			Apennine landscape with physical/natural characteristics and historical/cultural elements spread throughout the Valnerina	Apennine landscape with physical/natural characteristics in the Martani and Amerino Mountains	Apennine landscape with physical/natural characteristics in the Martani and Amerino Mountains
A. NATURAL SYSTEM	1	Regeneration of forest landscapes, favouring structural diversity	✓	✓	✓
	2	Managing the renaturalization of mountain meadows	✓	✓	
	3	Protection of wet environments and waterways	✓		
	4	Reinforcing bands of natural vegetation along rivers and in plains			✓
B. RURAL SYSTEM	1	Protection of traditional agrarian landscapes characterized by a mosaic of forests and cultivation		✓	
	2	Protection of residual cultivated mountain landscapes	✓		
	3	Regeneration of rural valley landscapes			✓
	4	Maintenance and restructuring of portions of rural territory where high-quality farming persists and/or specialized production chains arise, in order to counteract the abandonment of cultivated areas			✓
C. SETTLEMENT SYSTEM	1	Protection of residual areas with high biological value by regenerating degraded contexts and adjacent areas			
	2	Enhancing the relationship between historical towns and the natural/rural context	✓	✓	
	3	Regeneration of the urban-rural continuum in peri-urban areas			✓
	4	Urban regeneration through interventions to renaturalize and penetrate the natural structure in settled areas			

Tab.1 Strategic actions for the different landscape areas in Umbria Region

[Hill]y landscapes			Valley and lake landscapes			
…cape …ith …tural …ics	Hilly landscape of Orvieto with historical/cultural characteristics	Hilly landscape with physical/natural characteristics in the low Tiber Valley	Lake landscape of Lake Trasimeno with physical/natural characteristics	Valley landscape of Perugia with social/symbolic characteristics	Valley landscape of the Umbra Valley with social/symbolic characteristics	Valley landscape of Conca Ternana with social/symbolic characteristics
	✓			✓		✓
					✓	
		✓	✓			✓
	✓	✓				✓
	✓	✓	✓		✓	✓
		✓	✓		✓	
					✓	✓
				✓		✓
	✓	✓	✓	✓	✓	✓
				✓	✓	✓
				✓	✓	✓

semi-natural environment can gradually be modified and "contaminate" the settlement structure of marginal areas, aiming to activate processes to regenerate and enhance the most critical areas.

- *Lake landscape of Lake Trasimeno with physical/natural characteristics*
- *Valley landscape of Perugia with social/symbolic characteristics*
- *Valley landscape of the Umbra Valley with social/symbolic characteristics*
- *Valley landscape of Conca Ternana with social/symbolic characteristics*

The table in the previous page lists the strategic actions that have been identified for each landscape in Umbria.

References

- Cinquini F., Perna P., Sargolini M. (a cura di) (2006). *Reti ecologiche e siti natura 2000.* di Sargolini Cinquini Perna. vol. 1, p. 1-223, Roma: Edizioni Kappa, ISBN: 9788878907423
- Sargolini M. (2006). *La rete ecologica per gestire le interazioni tra l'uomo e la natura. Il caso studio della regione marche.* in: WWF Italia. Conservazione ecoregionale, reti ecologiche e governo del territorio. Atti del convegno nazionale del giugno 2005. vol. 1, p. 61-63, Roma: WWF Italia
- Sargolini M. (2007). *La dimensione ecologica del paesaggio.* in: Battisti C. e Romano B.. *Frammentazione e connettività.* vol. 1, p. 376-379, Novara: de Agostini Scuola Spa, ISBN: 9788825173147
- Sargolini M. (a cura di) (2008). *La pianificazione delle aree protette nelle marche. Uno studio di casi.* vol. 51, p. 1-184, Roma: Inu Edizioni, ISBN: 9788876030277
- Caprodossi R., Gamberoni C., Perna P., Sargolini M. (2009). *Aree dismesse e rete ecologica.* in: Barbieri P. (a cura di). Hyper Adriatica. OP2 Opere pubbliche e citta' adriatica. vol. Unico, p. 266-273, Barcellona: LISt lab Laboratorio Internazionala Editoriale, ISBN: 9788895623177
- Sargolini M. (2011). *All'origine di tutto. Reti ecologiche nella pianificazione dei parchi e delle aree contigue..* in: Falqui E., Calamita F. e Pavoni P. . Paesaggio, luogo della mente. p. 541-566, pisa: edizioni ets, ISBN: 9788846730503
- Morandi F., Niccolini F., Sargolini M. (2012). Parks and Territory. New perspective in planning organization. p. 1-201, Barcellona: LISt lab Laboratorio Internazionala Editoriale, ISBN: 9788895623788
- Sargolini M., (2012). *Urban Landscape. Environmental networks and quality of life.* p. 1-178, Milano: Springer-Verlag, ISBN: 9788847028791
- Caprodossi R., Pierantoni I., Sargolini M., (2015) *Reti ambientali, itinerari lauretani e comunità locali*; in Marca/Marche, 4/2015; pp.: 99-114; Andrealivi Editore. ISSN:2284-0389
- Caprodossi R., Sargolini M., (2015). *La rete ecologica regionale per la rigenerazione urbana. Il caso studio del conero.* pp.: 108-117. in: Voghera a. (a cura di), Progetti per il paesaggio. libro in memoria di attilia peano. Inu Edizioni. ISBN: 978-88-7603-134-2
- Sargolini M., (2016). C'è un futuro per le aree protette ?. in: Moccia d., Sepe M., . Reti e infrastrutture dei territori contemporanei. p. 187-197, Roma: Inu Edizioni, ISBN: 9788876031472

Promoting green jobs related to the Natura 2000 Network

Tania Deodati, Marco Gisotti

Comunità Ambiente

Among the large objectives, the management strategy identified the promotion of green jobs ties to the Natura 2000 Network, organized in turn into seven specific objectives:

1. Professional training tied to quality food and agricultural systems compatible with the environment. The success of agricultural activities and the agricultural industry is increasingly tied to a capacity to produce healthy, genuine foods while respecting the environment. The most requested professional figures may therefore be tied to the development of organic agriculture, but also to conventional agriculture with environmentally friendly methods that are attentive to the quality of the product.

2. Professional training tied to the sustainable management of forest systems. The trend for the sustainable management of forest systems, made through afforestation, the reconstruction of forests damaged by fires, the realization of infrastructure and equipment to prevent fires, or interventions for renaturalization, contribute to the maintenance and vitality of forest ecosystems, promoting professional training for foresters and advanced education in forest planning.

3. Professional training tied to environmental tourism. The growing attention for environmental tourism, the search for emotionally enriching experiences (from the visual, auditory, and gustatory points of view) that entail learning (e.g., teaching farms) or express a social commitment (active ethical vacations with a social or ecological contribution) increase the request for professions such as nature guides, experts in environmental education, etc.

4. Professional training tied to cultural and recreational activities in the Natura 2000 Network. The combination of nature and culture, which is particularly strong and present in Umbria, can be the source of new professional activities tied to reading the landscape, teaching about the local cultural heritage, approaching ancient skills that have disappeared, rediscovering popular songs, ecomuseums, etc.

5. Professional training tied to the sustainable management of aquatic systems. Aquatic systems offer opportunities tied to green jobs, promoting the training of aspiring professional fishermen and teaching about fishing and tourism.

6. Promotion of green jobs in schools and universities. To create an effective green educational program, a series of interventions for orientation, communication, and policy aimed at the various players is necessary: students, teachers, and universities in the region. The opportunity to make use of the school-work program represents another opportunity for orientation and knowledge about the Natura 2000 Network.

7. Promotion of policy activities to promote green jobs. Supporting green professions requires rapport-building to find the numerous players to participate in the creation, management, and training of green workers.

Objective 8

Improving awareness and information about the value of the Natura 2000 Network and ecosystem services

Cristiano Spilinga, Francesca Montioni, Silvia Carletti, Emi Petruzzi

Studio Naturalistico Hyla

This objective foresees the implementation of information regarding the value of the Natura 2000 Network for the greater public and economic operators by developing ad hoc communication strategies for the various targets identified.

To improve knowledge and information about the value of the Natura 2000 Network for the greater public, various actions were identified starting with the design of a communication campaign that in turn establishes a categorization of the actions in relation to the reference targets identified.

In addition to classical communication channels (websites, blogs newsletters, events, materials), other tools were identified that foresee the targets' active involvement thanks to direct experiences that can be had within the areas comprising the Natura 2000 Network. These include environmental education activities aimed at schools, citizen science projects (entailing the involvement and active participation of citizens in collecting information and scientific data), and the creation of trekking maps and guides, as well as innovative tools for the enjoyment of the areas.

Another priority objective identified in the management strategy is to raise the public's awareness about alien species, considering that an important role in their spread is played by the market of ornamental plants and pets, the voluntary introduction for sport fishing and hunting, the release by citizens, and animals escaping from farms and zoos.

In this view, the population's involvement is first and foremost, by reinforcing environmental education and scientific disclosure.

Another objective is to improve knowledge and information about the value of the Natura 2000 Network with economic players. The areas in the Natura 2000 Network are in fact not rigidly protected reserves that exclude human activities; the protection of nature intends to be guaranteed also "taking account of economic, social, cultural, and regional requirements". One of the main tools identified to reach the objective is the creation of a synthetic manual aimed at economic players in which the characteristics of the Natura 2000 Network are briefly illustrated, along with the potential of creating territorial marketing and the capacity for financing thanks to European funds specifically aimed at these areas.

In addition, the activation of educational paths, seminars, and internships aimed at communicating the opportunities that the green economy and green jobs offer in terms of greater employment and probability of business success within the Natura 2000 Network sites can provide tools and knowledge useful for creating green businesses.

Another objective of the management strategy is to improve knowledge and information about the value of ecosystem services tied to the presence of the Natura 2000 Network.

The communication campaign aimed at increasing knowledge and awareness of the value of ecosystem services should be directed both at the general public and at economic players, with particular reference to the agricultural sectors.

Specifically, the possibility of labelling products produced sustainably and obtained thanks to the ecosystem services offered by the natural environment would not only allow the services themselves to be recognized, but it would also favour the local economy.

In addition, the ecosystem services applied to agriculture (agro-ecosystem services) can represent a primary means to communicate the importance of biodiversity, with its effectiveness through activities to inform, train, and educate children and adults, leading to a new cultural and behavioural trend that will lead to greater and more complex awareness and knowledge about biodiversity and problems tied to its loss.

References

- Ercole S., Giacanelli V., Bacchetta G., Fenu G., Genovesi P. (Eds.), 2016. Manuali per il monitoraggio di specie e habitat di interesse comunitario (Direttiva 92/43/CEE) in Italia: specie vegetali. ISPRA, Serie Manuali e linee guida, 140/2016.
- Angelini P., Casella L., Grignetti A., Genovesi P., 2016. Manuali per il monitoraggio di specie e habitat di interesse comunitario (Direttiva 92/43/CEE) in Italia: habitat. ISPRA, Serie Manuali e Linee Guida, 142/2016.
- Stoch F., Genovesi P., 2016. Manuali per il monitoraggio di specie e habitat di interesse comunitario (Direttiva 92/43/CEE) in Italia: specie animali. ISPRA, Serie Manuali e linee guida, 141/2016

The new financial plan for managing the Natura 2000 Network

Carla Cortina, Lucia Rocchi, Antonio Boggia

DSA3, University of Perugia

The Natura 2000 Network, in order to maintain the habitats and species in a favourable state of conservation and be adequately managed, requires sufficient financial resources. To respect the obligations related to the adoption of conservation measures, the member states should necessarily sustain the costs that, in theory, should be covered by their national budgets according to subsidiarity. However, Art. 8 of the Habitats Directive provides European co-financing for these activities when necessary. In a specific Communication[1], the European Commission (EC) first considered strengthening and perfecting the LIFE-Natura tool to make it the principal mechanism of financing the Natura 2000 Network. It therefore evaluated the possibility of creating a new tool specifically destined for financing the Natura 2000 Network, but then proposed that co-financing be adopted within existing financing tools. The goal of the Commission's choice was threefold: ensure that management of the Natura 2000 Network sites was part of broader territorial management policies; allow member states to identify priorities and develop policies and measures that reflect their national and regional characteristics; and avoid duplication and overlapping of different European financing tools.

The development of the 2017–2023 financing plan (FP) to manage the Natura 2000 Network in Umbria preliminarily required the drafting of a report on the costs of the network in the 2007–2013 period of structural fund planning (referring to the effective period in which the funds were used, i.e., 2008–2015) and an estimate of the annual costs to manage the network in the period 2017–2023.

The analysis of the type of activities financed to provide for the needs of the Natura 2000 Network using the available funds (mainly European) during the past planning of structural funds (2001–2013) was useful. It clarified the type of interventions made, the funds used, and possible problems that arose. In addition, it allowed for an evaluation of the effectiveness of the management and the interventions that were financed.

Overall spending for the Natura 2000 Network in the period 2008–2015 (2001–2013 planning) was equal to €59,736,448, equal to an average annual spending of €7,467,056. Therefore, the average annual spending per hectare was about €57. This is lower than the €63/ha/yr for Natura 2000 Network sites on land in the 27 member states (IEEP, 2010), an average of very different amounts of spending among the countries. The average annual

---

1. COM(2004) 431 def.

amount for Umbria, equal to €57/ha, is closest to the annual €53/ha for the Lombardy Region for the 2010–2011 period (LIFE+ GESTIRE).

Sixty-seven percent of spending on the Natura 2000 Network came from the Regional Development Programme (RDP) and nearly 48% came specifically from Measure 214 "Agricultural/environmental payments"; about 13% came from the Regional Operational Programme (ROP) ERDF; nearly 10% from LIFE+ Programmes; about 6% from the Regional Implementation Program (RIP) under the Fund for Development and Cohesion; a little more than 1% from the Ministry of the Environment and the Protection of the Land and Sea; and about 2.6% from regional funds under the Regional Fauna Observatory. Graph 1 shows the distribution of overall spending for each year. The spending was concentrated in the central years, with the highest annual spending reaching €91/ha in 2013, followed by €79/ha in 2011, and €75/ha in 2012.

The costs were reclassified as ordinary management costs, costs for conservation, investment, and monitoring, and in reference to 12 of the 25 types of management activities identified by the EU[2].

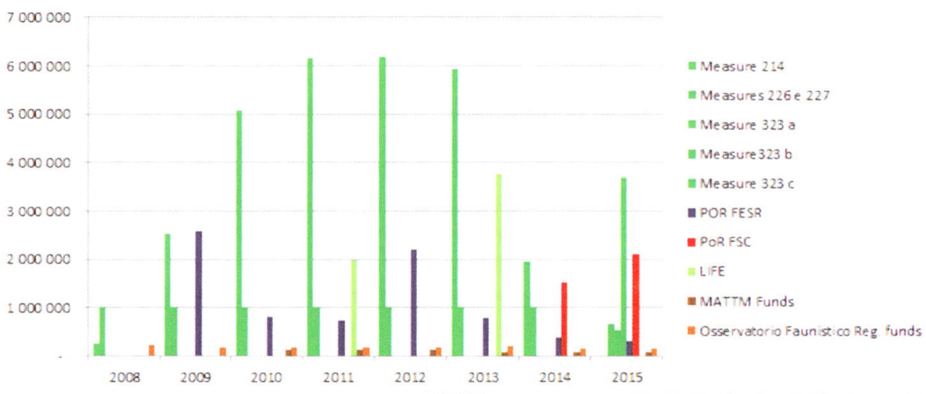

Graf.1 Spending for the Natura 2000 Network from various funds in the 2008–2015 period (euros).

2. These are management activities established by the Commission under Annex 3 of the Communication on financing the Natura 2000 Network COM (2004) 431 final. In the case of costs in the 2007–2013 period, 12 were considered since the first 11 foresee activities related to designating the Natura 2000 Network sites and the development of management plans, activities that were already completed using funds in the previous planning period. However, these were all considered again in the financial plan to better predict the revision of the management plan.2020" (EC, 2014-2) e 'Financing Rete Natura 2000: Analysis of Rete Natura 2000 management measures eligible for financing Rete Natura 2000' (EC, 2014-2)

In the regional financing plan for the strategy to manage the Natura 2000 Network in Umbria, both the active part (resources potentially available to finance the Natura 2000 Network) and the passive part (costs to satisfy the need to manage the Natura 2000 Network) were estimated.

The first part identifies all the possible sources of financing for the Natura 2000 Network. For European Structural and Investment (ESI) Funds with indirect management, the indications contained in the Commission guidelines[3] were crossed with the regional programs related to EAFRD, ERDF, and ESF. With regard to the programmes, this enabled a selection to be made of those measures/actions that could potentially be combined to finance the Natura 2000 Network. This allowed matrices to be produced of the sources of financing for each fund. The analysis for Umbria's RDP EAFRD reached the level of sub-measure, allowing the potentially available gross amounts to be better detailed (Figure 2).

The framework related to the possible channels of financing the Natura 2000 Network was completed by considering the contribution from direct management funds dealt with in another document.

The passive part of the financial plan, i.e., the overall cost of interventions expected from the regional strategic design for the Natura 2000 Network, was estimated with reference to the costs sustained for the Natura 2000 Network in the past and the greater availability of funds today. The total was equal to €78 million for the 2017–2023 period. The annual cost of managing the Network was determined to be equal to €11 million. This corresponds to €85.9/ha/yr and is on the order of what was estimated by the European Commission as the annual management cost (€80/ha/yr) to effectively conserve biodiversity[4].

3. These are European guides "Financing Rete Natura 2000: EU funding opportunities in 2014-2020" (EC, 2014-2) and "Financing Rete Natura 2000: Analysis of Rete Natura 2000 management measures eligible for financing Rete Natura 2000" (EC, 2014-2).

4. http://www.be-natur.it/downloads/Be-Natur_WP3_1-%20FINAL_Gap-Analysis.pdf (last accessed on 18/04/2018)

Umbrian EAFRD RDP 2014-2020 measures	Sub-measures	Euro (000)	1	2	3	4	5	6	7	8	9	10	11	12	13	14	15	16	17	18	19	20	21	22	23	24	25
M01	1.1	600			X																		X				
	1.2	200			X																		X				
	1.3	55			X																		X				
M02	2.1	470																					X				
	2.3	30																					X				
M04	4.4	4,000												X	X	X		X						X		X	
M07	7.1	8,500			X		X			X																	
M07	7.5	14,000										X												X			X
M07	7.6	18,000												X	X	X											
M08	8.1	16,000												X	X	X											
M08	8.2	1,000												X	X	X											
M08	8.3	24,000												X	X	X				X							
	8.4	1,000												X	X	X				X							
M08	8.5	25,000												X	X	X				X							
M10	10.1	126,500												X	X	X	X	X									
	10.2	3,000												X	X	X	X	X									
M11	11.1	4,000												X	X		X										
	11.2	30,100												X	X		X										
M12	12.1	5,000												X	X		X	X		X							
	12.2	1,000												X	X		X	X		X							
M13	13.1	40,000												X	X												
	13.2	23,000												X	X												
M15	15.1	2,000												X	X	X											
	15.2	3,000												X	X	X											
M16	16.5	1,000												X	X	X											
	16.8	1,000												X	X	X											
M19	19.4	28,000	X	X	X	X	X	X	X	X	X			X	X	X	X			X	X		X	X		X	X

Fig.2 Matrix of potential financing from the RDP EAFRD (2014–2020) for the 25 management activities.

The estimated costs were also ascribed to the 25 management activities established by the Commission and reclassified into the four categories of cost set out in the project.

Finally, the estimates made indicated an increase of about 30% in the costs necessary for the Natura 2000 Network in the 2017–2023 period over the 2007–2013 period.

Covering these costs with the funds examined is not certain because the sources of financing are not specifically for the Natura 2000 Network; the same sources of financing are called to cover more management activities and the funds are subordinate to the appropriate calls opened by the Umbria Region.

References

- (COM (2004) 431 def.) Parere del Comitato economico e sociale europeo in merito alla Comunicazione della Commissione al Consiglio e al Parlamento europeo: Finanziamento di Rete Natura 2000, http://eur-lex.europa.eu/legal-content/IT/TXT/PDF/?uri=CE-LEX:52005AE0136&from=IT
- COM (2013) 249 final "Infrastrutture verdi – Rafforzare il capitale naturale in Europa" http://ec.europa.eu/transparency/regdoc/rep/1/2013/IT/1-2013-249-IT-F1-1.Pdf
- Commission Communication on the financing of Rete Natura 2000 COM (2004) 431 final. http://eurlex.europa.eu/legalcontent/EN/TXT/PDF/?uri=CELEX:-52004DC0431&from=EN
- EC, 2005. Financing Rete Natura 2000: Guidance Handbook, ENV B.2/SER/2005/0020
- EC, 2013. The economic benefits of the Rete Natura 2000 Network. http://ec.europa.eu/environment/nature/natura2000/financing/docs/ENV-12-018_LR_Final1.pdf
- EC, 2014 (1). Financing Rete Natura 2000: Guidance Handbook, EU funding opportunities ISBN 978-92-79-38604-6: Publications Office of the EU, Luxembourg
- EC, 2014 (2). Analysis of Rete Natura 2000 management measures eligible for financing in 2014-2020. Financing Rete Natura 2000: Guidance Handbook, ISBN 978-92-79-38632-9, Publications Office of the EU, Luxembourg
- Gantioler S., Rayment M., Bassi S., Kettunen M., McConville A., Landgrebe R., Gerdes H, ten Brink P. *Costs and Socio-Economic Benefits associated with the Rete Natura 2000 Network. Final report to the European Commission,* DG Environment on Contract ENV.B.2/SER/2008/0038. Institute for European Environmental Policy / GHK / Ecologic, Brussels 2010
- Gatto P., Maso D., Leonardi A., 2015. Analisi dei costi per la gestione della Rete Natura 2000 in Regione Lombardia nel periodo 2008-2011 e di stima dei costi nel periodo 2014-2020 ETIFOR Srl –Spin-off dell'Università di Padova. (LIFE11NAT/IT/044 GESTIRE)

Updating the PAF

Livia Bellisari, Tania Deodati

Comunità Ambiente

The PAF (Priority Action Framework) is a strategic tool for multi-annual planning aimed at determining a complete overview of the measures necessary to activate the Natura 2000 Network and the related green infrastructure, specifying the need for financing for these measures and tying them to the corresponding financing programmes.
In line with the objectives of the European Habitats Directive, the basis of the Natura 2000 Network, the measures to be identified in the PAFs are mainly designed "to maintain or restore, at favourable conservation status, natural habitats and species of wild fauna and flora of Community interest … [taking] account of economic, social and cultural requirements and regional and local characteristics" (Art. 2 Habitats Directive).
In particular, the PAF responds to the obligations established in Art. 8 of the Directive, which requires member states to send the European Commission their own estimates regarding the co-financing necessary to implement the Natura 2000 Network. In fact, according to Art. 6 of the Directive, member states should "establish the necessary conservation meas-ures involving, if need be, appropriate management plans specifically designed for the sites or integrated into other development plans, and appropriate statutory, administrative or contractual measures which correspond to the ecological requirements of the natural habitat types in Annex I and the species in Annex II present on the sites".
The PAF therefore focuses on identifying those needs and priorities for direct financing tied to the specific measures of conservation established for the Natura 2000 Network sites in order to reach the objectives of conservation on the site level for those species and habitats for which the site was designated. Since the Natura 2000 Network also includes Special Protection Areas (SPA) designated under EU Directive 2009/147/EEC Birds Directive, the PAF also considers the need for financing and the priority measures associated with bird species in the SPAs.
More recently, in the conclusions to the EU Action Plan for nature, people, and the economy[1],

---

1. http://www.consilium.europa.eu/en/press/press-releases/2017/06/19/conclusions-eu-action-plan-nature/

the European Union recognizes the need to further improve multi-year financial planning for investments in nature and agrees on the need to update and improve the PAFs. The importance of better foreseeing the needs of financing the Natura 2000 Network in view of the EU's next multi-year financial framework was also recognized by the European Parliament in a specific resolution[2].

In addition, the priority measures identified under the PAFs contribute not only to the specific objectives of the EU's directive on nature, but also provides important benefits for socioeconomic and ecosystem services, such as the mitigation of and adaptation to climate change and the development of tourism and culture.

In Italy, the PAFs were developed by the Regions and some, including Umbria, requested and obtained financing under the LIFE+ Programme in order to develop a more detailed and precise plan of action and the related sources of financing. Thanks to these funds, the PAF was one of two main objectives of the SUN LIFE project.

The Umbria Region already had a PAF, and DGR no. 323 of 15/04/2013 approved the PAF for the Natura 2000 Network in Umbria for the 2014–2020 period.

Under the SUN LIFE project, it was therefore necessary to update the PAF based on the investigations made during the project and taking account of the conclusions of the discussion regarding financing tools for the Natura 2000 Network.

An integral part of the PAF lies in identifying potential sources of financing, with a view to integrating economic resources. For example, the PAF can expect to mobilize direct European funds to realize the priority actions, such as financing from the LIFE Programme, funds for fishing (EMFF) or research (Horizon 2020), structural funds, e.g., funds for rural development (EAFRD), society (ESF), or even national or private funds.

The definition of priorities for financing will allow the limited financial resources available to be best used to manage the Natura 2000 Network and facilitate its ability to reach the objectives of conservation for habitats and species in a reasonable period of time, contributing significantly to activating the EU Strategy on Biodiversity for 2020 – Our life insurance, our natural capital.

---

2. European Parliament resolution of 15 November 2017 on an Action Plan for nature, people and the economy (2017/2819(RSP)) http://www.europarl.europa.eu/sides/getDoc.do?type=TA&language=EN&reference=P8-TA-2017-0441

Guidelines for farmers and foresters

Daniela Gigante, Enzo Goretti, Gianandrea La Porta, Massimo Lorenzoni, Fabio Maneli, Matteo Pallottini, Laura Pompei, Manuela Rebora, Roberto Venanzoni

DCBB, University of Perugia

Maintaining the delicate balance between environmental protection, social needs, and economic activities is one of the main cornerstones of the current approach to biodiversity conservation. In Umbria, forestry and agriculture are extremely important, widespread activities, so the area of the C4 action in the SUN LIFE project was established to develop two guides specifically aimed at foresters and farmers. These guides do not aim to be strategic planning documents for agricultural and forestry activities and contain no legislative characteristics, but rather offer orientations for good practices to apply the regulations in European Directives to conserve biodiversity: the Habitats Directive (92/43/EEC) and the Birds Directive (2009/147/EEC).

The main causes of biodiversity degradation include the improper use of biotic resources and the abandonment of the territories, which, especially in the case of the secondary grassy Habitats, are giving rise to rapid transformations. In this scenario, farmers and foresters could play a key role in restoring, directing, and implementing some forms of traditional land use that would allow for their protection and guarantee the conservation of landscapes and their use, as well as their undeniable historical/cultural value. The main purpose of the two guides is therefore to make farmers and foresters aware of the problems in the Natura 2000 Network, explaining simply and immediately what their contribution could be in conserving biodiversity while they go about their daily production activities.

The Guide for Foresters aims to illustrate the role of forests and forestry in the Natura 2000 Network in Umbria and to provide the main users of forest resources with information and advice to best manage forestry activities in view of their sustainable use. In fact, a forestry intervention, even with the purposes of improvement, can lead to a short- and long-term impact on the biotic and abiotic components of the ecosystem and in particular, on plant and animal communities and the land. Sometimes just small precautions are enough to reduce environmental impact and increase the sustainability of the interventions. In this guide, 12 good forestry practices are proposed to contribute to conserving the forest Habitats in Annex I, expedients that can help to improve the state of health of the forests in Umbria and in particular those present within Natura 2000 Network sites. In particular, the good practices regard the following themes: performing varied interventions, interventions over small surface areas, conversions and transformations, maintaining the diversity of tree species, increasing structural diversity, releasing large trees, releasing dead trees and dead wood on the ground, releasing bushes, periods of intervention, methods for concentrating and thinning forests, management of reforesting, and creation of forests and reforesting.

In a similar way, the Guide for Farmers aims to illustrate the role of farming in the Natura 2000 Network in Umbria and to provide farmers with information and advice to manage agricultural activities in a view of environmental sustainability. Eleven good agricultural practices are proposed to contribute to conserving biodiversity, which regard the following themes: working the land, diversifying crops, irrigation, agrarian hydraulic systems, buffer hedges and bands/lines of bushes, fertilization, plant-health interventions, seed preservation, crops being lost, pasture management, and management of permanent stable fields.

For each good practice proposed, the guides describe the means and times of execution and provide references to existing laws and possible associated financing to carry out the activities. In addition, the Habitats in Annex I and the animal and plant species in Annexes II, IV, and V in the Habitats Directive and the birds in Annex I of the Birds Directive are indicated, along with which good practice will affect them directly or indirectly.

The two guides also provide general information about the Natura 2000 Network in Umbria, accompanied by photographs and maps, including tables of the SACs and SPAs present in the Region. The guides contain a focus on the SUN LIFE project and a general description of the objectives of the project and the partners involved.

3.5

Interventions to support jobs in managing and enhancing the Natura 2000 Network

Marco Gisotti, Oliviero Spinelli

Comunità Ambiente

In general, with regard for the professions more or less closely tied to the management and enhancement of the Natura 2000 Network areas, a lack of relationships between actors and territorial operators was revealed over the course of the project. There is a broad range of skills that have the useful capacity of bringing citizens to the Natura 2000 Network as well as the greater system of protected areas and nature conservation, considering that even areas of only cultural or orientation skills can be developed in non-specific sectors.

For example, in their role as social facilitators in their mediation activities between business and territory and institutions, anthropologists could find interesting margins of professional success. Another example is the need to stimulate involvement and effective interaction between players in tourism on the regional level and individual subjects that currently act and work autonomously, where concerted plans for communication and territorial networking would be necessary.

Protected areas and the Natura 2000 Network can serve as gravitational centres for a territorial system where valuable skills and experiences already exist, but which should, however be implemented through a steering committee. Over the course of the project, it was observed, in fact, how Umbria lacks an organic system of services for tourists that allows the best possible offer with the prestige of environmental resources to be reached.

The same could be said for other sectors, such as multi-functional agriculture, the commercial network, the sectors of waste and energy, and the energy efficiency of human activities present in the territory, including the regeneration of urban settlements.

It is understood that the integration of new or renewed professional figures related to these fields is necessary where businesses and institutions have reorganized their activities along these lines. It is not enough for the job market to take on professionals oriented at greening before the educational needs are expressed, but it is necessary that the two times (request for professionals and education) coincide.

There are anyway tools to determine professional needs, such as the Excelsior Information System by ANPAL (National Agency for Active Work Policies) and Unioncamere, which, on a provincial level, are able to provide a dynamic and constantly updated framework with regard to businesses.

A process to support professions to manage and enhance the Natura 2000 Network should therefore be distributed over at least three distinct but concerted instances: policy, orientation, and education.

"Policy" intends the support of those institutional and socioeconomic processes among the various actors capable of creating active work policies, orientating professions and skills in the direction of a green economy that includes processes of wildlife economy and circular economy. This means activities for interaction, mediation, and study among institutions and groups of subjects in society, such as labour unions, professional and employment associations, environmental groups, universities and research groups, chambers of commerce, etc.

Exchanging experiences and highlighting reciprocal and specific needs is in fact capable of initiating those policies, which are aimed at more effective interventions during legislation and regulation, activation, and use of lines of financing and territorial policies in general. In this view, the main actor is naturally the Region, which, through its regulatory organs, can require and is required to carry out a series of promotion activities – both at no cost and with ad hoc financing – that build activity cycles in the form, for example, of annual thematic campaigns and that periodically involve the different territorial players.

"Orientation" implies the cultural interventions necessary to orient both individual behaviour through knowledge and information, and the individual propensity for sustainability in a transverse manner in professional areas.

In the chain of professions, it is important to consider not only the schools that are clearly closest to the themes of conservation and territorial management, but also those fields of knowledge that are apparently widely separated but cooperate and provide elements of economy or management (economics, law, humanities, education science, etc.).

Finally, "education" means the real, direct, and/or organizational support for educational activities, at least in the five areas identified (environmentally friendly and quality food and agricultural systems, cultural and recreational activities, sustainable management of aquatic systems).

This support can be achieved thanks to policy activities and concretization through, for example, interventions in favour of educational projects in the 2014–2020 catalogue – ESF Axis 1 Inclusive labour markets, specifically for profiles related to green jobs, inserting educational modules explicitly oriented towards Natura 2000 Network areas and nature conservation.

The direct involvement of the Ministry of Education, Universities, and Research will be important for technical working groups in which specialists, technicians, teachers, and businesses will participate to promote school-work projects oriented at green jobs.

Just as the educational world can benefit from seminars, working tables, and conferences promoted by the Region for the operators of the employment agencies and work orientation centres in Umbria, Regional entities accredited in providing educational courses financed by the ESF will also be involved in designing courses with employment outlets in green jobs.

3.6

Priority projects

ECORETE

Daniela Gigante, Enzo Goretti, Gianandrea La Porta, Massimo Lorenzoni, Fabio Maneli, Matteo Pallottini, Laura Pompei, Manuela Rebora, Roberto Venanzoni

DCBB, University of Perugia

Alessandro Marucci, Francesco Zullo, Lorena Fiorini, Bernardino Romano

DICEAA, University of L'Aquila

Over the course of the SUN LIFE project, through an examination of the heritage of species and Habitats included in the regional Natura 2000 Network, a management strategy was implemented that, based on the current state of conservation and the species- and habitat-specific management needs, identified the priorities for action on the regional scale. These priorities view some Habitats[1] and species tied to the aquatic and plain environments in circumstances of maximum risk. Here, more than in other areas, the problem of environmental fragmentation, the reduction of bio-permeability, and impacts caused by AISs are accentuated.

This context frames the activities established in the LIFE ECORETE pilot project, formulated and proposed within the SUN LIFE project, which grew out of the need to mitigate the effects of fragmentation on ecological populations, communities, and processes in order to create an interconnected system of habitats. The LIFE project aims to construct an organic tool to guarantee the activation of management, conservation, and monitoring measures identified in the PAF for the Habitats and species in the regional Natura 2000 Network in the strategic areas that present an elevated risk of transformation and degradation.

The disappearance of Habitats due to transformations in land use and the fragmentation of residual areas constitute one of the main threats to biodiversity. Among the consequences of fragmentation are contraction, isolation, floral impoverishment, and the disappearance of Habitats, an increase in the surface area of human types of land use, an increase in the level of "contrast", and the effective margin between Habitat and non-Habitat, with very profound impacts on biodiversity. These phenomena influence the structure and population dynamics of numerous animal and plant species, and wind up altering the composition of the communities, ecosystem functions, and ecological processes. It was also demonstrated how, on the species level, this process constitutes one of the causes of the current high rate of extinction worldwide. The maintenance/restoration of ecological connectivity therefore represents a fundamental action for conserving Habitats and species, in particular those that are most sensitive to fragmentation (in general stenoecious species and those tied to specific biological habitats, those that are rather stationary or, on the contrary, those that require different habitats at different moments in their life cycle) and for which processes of isolation can be identified. The strengthening or restoration of bio-permeability also represents one of the key elements in managing and mitigating the negative effects caused by climate change. One of the most predictable responses to rising temperatures will consist, in fact, in an attempt to follow the optimal temperature, with the displacement of entire populations in latitude (northwards) and altitude (up the mountains).

The project is organized into two specific areas of intervention: subaerial and aquatic environments. By virtue of their different characteristics, they each require a series of different actions, with the common objective of providing fragmented ecosystems with the conditions necessary to maintain the vitality of the populations in the long term.

With regard to the subaerial environment, the SUN LIFE project made an in-depth recognition of the main infrastructure in the Region, developing "profiles of ecosystem occlusion". This led to a census of the discontinuities due to fragmentation caused by roads (gaps) that could potentially constitute "effective" ecological connections for biotic flows. The available data allow some specific steps to be implemented in order to detail the aspects of efficiency for fauna and the characteristics of the environmental matrix in which the gaps are found.

1. In the text, "Habitat" will be capitalized to indicate the habitats included in Annex I of Directive 92/43/EEC..

The problem of territorial fragmentation and the consequent rarefaction of biological habitats is very significant in some territorial contexts, such as the wide river valleys or plains where anthropization is greater and the plant communities are consequently more compromised. At the same time, they represent one of the main natural infrastructures through which biotic flows are concretized in subaerial areas. As well, in these territorial contexts, the recomposition of original plant communities would also be very significant from the conservation point of view, since they are strongly rarefied or even absent in the regional territory. In particular, these territorial compartments present the potential of vegetation for southern ash and English, sessile, and Italian oak forests, which are found regionally in various Habitats in Annex I (e.g., 91E0*, 91M0, 92A0, 91F0) but which have currently almost or completely disappeared.

With regard to the aquatic environment, its particular characteristics impose unique conditions of existence on flora and fauna that are more limited with respect to what is experienced by organisms on land. Rivers are essentially linear systems (river corridors) in which movement occurs in a single direction and with a preferential sense towards the valley caused by the presence of the current. The dispersion of fish species and plant propagation is therefore possible only within the natural connections of the hydrographical network: the water environments are therefore characterized by a high degree of isolation. Waterways and wet areas constitute a uniform system that plays an essential role of innervating the entire regional territory and hosting numerous species of flora and fauna that are now rarefied and, for some groups of fauna, endemic, very often rare, or threatened.

With particular regard for fish, the main factors limiting ecological connectivity of the populations within the hydrographical network are, firstly, dams and small barriers that, lacking steps for climbing, constitute insurmountable barriers, especially in the case of reduced flows and for species with little vagility. Obstacles to free circulation are not only physical, but also include sections of polluted water or insufficient waterflow, for example, which act as barriers for aquatic organisms. In this sense, integration with the Water Framework Directive (WFD, 2000/60 CE), which institutes a framework for European action in matters of water systems in order to prevent the qualitative and quantitative deterioration of aquatic ecosystems. For the aquatic and river Habitats, the main causes of fragmentation undoubtedly include proximity to agricultural, urban, and industrial areas, which are hardly ever mitigated by the presence of buffer zones. The effects of this contact are both direct – through the removal of phytocenoses (which already due to their intrinsic needs tend to develop in more or less narrow bands as a function of the water gradient) – and indirect – entering the polluted and biocidal environment and provoking the settlement of ubiquitous and synanthropic species. Finally, a general cause of fragmentation and degradation is represented by exotic species, particularly AISs. In the case of species capable of cross-breeding with indigenous species, genetic exchange between populations is interrupted, leading to the disappearance of populations with different levels of genetic introgression. In the case of Habitats, some AISs now stably settled on the regional level (e.g., Robinia pseudoacacia) have already greatly altered the flora, structure, and ecosystem of plant communities, in particular those in 92A0.

For the subaerial environment, the main objective of the LIFE ECORETE project consists in identifying and analysing the main key areas to maintain and restore the continuity of the Natura 2000 Network in Umbria. This will be achieved through several intermediate steps:

1. Selection of strategic gaps for regional environmental continuity. The selection of gaps will be realized by integrating qualitative/quantitative information related to the biotic flows between Natura 2000 Network areas, or between territorial areas with high conservation value because their interior contains areas of the Natura 2000 Network and/or national/regional parks. Starting with the action priorities related to the ecological continuity of the Natura 2000 Network, a hierarchy will therefore be contained within the PAF, assigning a coefficient of relative importance to each gap.
2. Context analysis. Standardization of the matrix buffer surrounding the selected gaps by analysing the regional geobotanical map and analysing the vegetation potential (Map of series of vegetation). The correct standardization of the environmental matrix associated with identification of the plants' importance leads to the development of multi-functional models for development/restoration/improvement of the strategic gaps, especially in cases where the potential plant communities are sparse or absent.
3. Specific analysis. Technical and functional characterization of the strategic gaps through advanced surveying procedures (GIS-UAV; 3D-HRM).
4. Monitoring the degree of compatibility of the content of municipal urban-planning tools and the functionality of the strategic gaps.
5. Formulation of possible proposals to modify/delocalize zones in order to reduce fragmentation.
6. Development and realization of projects for recovery, restoration, and expansion of the connections between Habitats by reconstructing the intermediate or mature stages of the series of vegetation in the territory of intervention through the use of local plant material.

For the aquatic environment, the project will identify the main problems that lead to the fragmentation of the regional hydrographical network, first making a census of and analysing the different types of obstacles that limit or interrupt river connectivity. This will allow specific plans for interventions to be developed within the project, taking account of the ecological characteristics (agility, size, life cycle duration, etc.) of the species that compose the fish communities and Habitats of interest. The project establishes specific actions aimed at recovering the ecological connectivity among populations of species of European interest within and between Natura 2000 Network sites, protected areas, and areas with high natural aspects. The numerous interventions foreseen under the project include an initial monitoring phase to update the data related to i) hydrology, by verifying the maintenance of the minimum vital flow, and ii) the genetics of some target species (Mediterranean trout, horse barbel), in order to assess the level of introgression and/or fragmentation of the populations. Particular importance will be reserved for monitoring AISs through integration with European regulation no. 1143/2014 of 22 October 2014 — Regulation on the prevention and management of the introduction and spread of invasive alien species. The main actions in this sense will see the development of Horizon scanning programmes; the creation of maps of permeability of the river and lake environments for invasive species present in the regional territory and for those that are likely to be introduced; the formulation of interventions to eradicate and/or contain AISs; the planning of actions to reintroduce target species (e.g., fish species such as the Mediterranean trout, horse barbel, and Arno goby), which also include the realization and adaptation of structures for the *ex situ* conservation and production of seed material; and the planning of recovery, restoration, and expansion activities for water Habitats through the use of local plant material. All the actions established in the project will contribute to realizing the primary objective, that is, improving the state of conservation of the species and Habitats of European interest by preserving and/or restoring the continuity of aquatic environments in Umbria, but also, where necessary, using the presence of obstacles to limit the expansion of AISs.

Analysis and assessment of the ecological effectiveness of the gaps

The work to recognize the potential ecological gaps in the main infrastructure system of the Region (nearly 100 gaps over about 380 km of roads and motorways) highlighted extremely varied conditions and notable localized criticalities: 51 water bypasses (5,300 m), 16 tunnels (13,150 m), 29 morphological bypasses (7,580 m), and more than 400 roadway underpasses (11,500 m) (Table 1). This structure determines a very complex panorama for which it is difficult to make simple generalizations. This analysis showed the unique aspect of the large barrier to land-based biotic flows represented by each category of the E45-Valtiberina, which basically breaks the Region's ecosystems into two east-west sections with very few really efficient or manageable connections. In the same way, other roadways cause significant, although apparently less drastic interruptions in complex infrastructure bands such as the Valle del Paglia (A1-TAV) and the Valtiberina mentioned above. Through a detailed examination of the discontinuities of the sections, it seemed rather clear that there really are a lot of crossings, several hundred among all the tracts studied, including water, morphological,

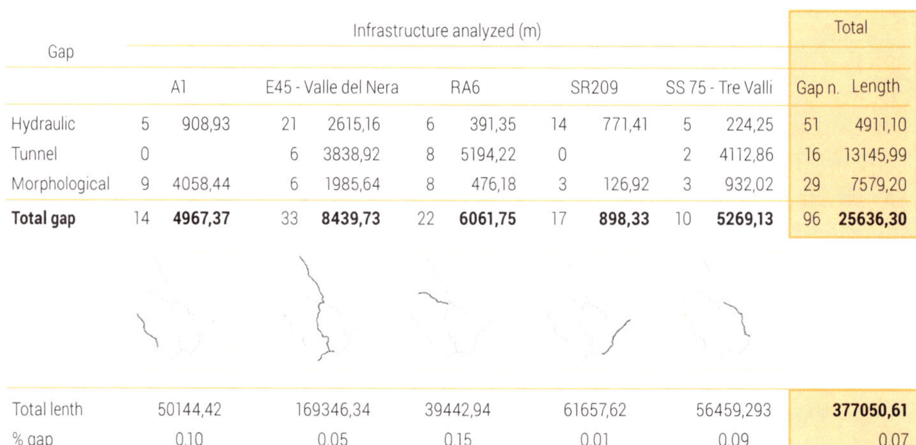

Gap		Infrastructure analyzed (m)										Total	
		A1		E45 - Valle del Nera		RA6		SR209		SS 75 - Tre Valli		Gap n.	Length
Hydraulic	5	908,93	21	2615,16	6	391,35	14	771,41	5	224,25		51	4911,10
Tunnel	0		6	3838,92	8	5194,22	0		2	4112,86		16	13145,99
Morphological	9	4058,44	6	1985,64	8	476,18	3	126,92	3	932,02		29	7579,20
Total gap	14	**4967,37**	33	**8439,73**	22	**6061,75**	17	**898,33**	10	**5269,13**		96	**25636,30**
Total lenth		50144,42		169346,34		39442,94		61657,62		56459,293			**377050,61**
% gap		0,10		0,05		0,15		0,01		0,09			0,07

Tab.1 A summary of the gaps in the regional infrastructure system

infrastructure bypasses and the exterior of tunnels. Therefore, a certain amount of biotic flux is statistically presumable, although there are no specific data on the species that use them and to what degree. The fact remains, however, that many of these permeabilities are made non-functional by the presence of dense linear urban areas that flank the roads and therefore generate significant physical/chemical disturbance for the potential movement of fauna. Table 1 also shows the distribution of the gaps on the roadways examined, considering only the hydraulic/river/morphological overpasses and the sections in tunnels, overlooking – as already mentioned – overpasses intersecting with other access ways.

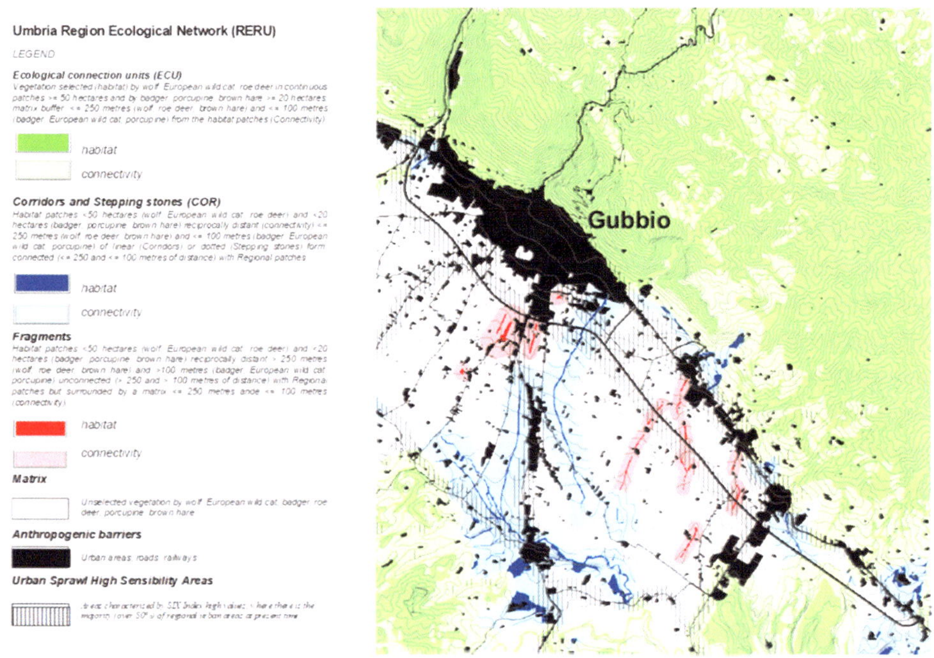

Fig.1 A portion of the institutional map of the Umbria Regional Ecological Network.

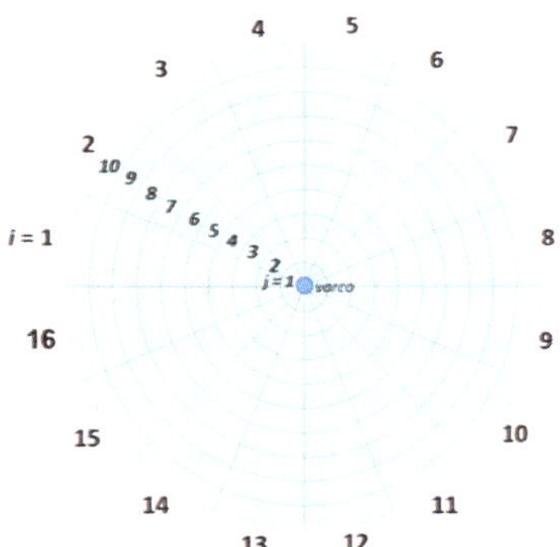

Fig.2 The radial grid centred on the gaps.

For the gaps selected, an efficiency index tied to the quality of the surrounding ecological matrix was then calculated. This quality derived from the map of the Umbria Regional Ecological Network (UREN) in Figure 1, which the Region has developed since 2000 (Ragni, 2009; Romano, 2004; van der Sluis & Pedroli, 2004 -http://library.wur.nl/WebQuery/wurpubs/fulltext/44982) and in which the ecological connection unit (ECU) and ecological corridors (COR) are identified. The matrix on which the efficiency of the gaps was measured derives from the presence of the two limiting spatial categories, but qualified as "habitat" (ECUCOR). A radial grid with a diameter of 20 km was traced around each gap (Figure 2). The grid was divided into 16 angular sections (i) and 19 radial buffers (j) of 1 km each. The grid was then crossed with ECUCOR to obtain the density of this matrix within each sector of the grid (Figure 3). The index of gap efficiency was then calculated as

where: $$GE = \sum_{i}^{8} = 1\,\frac{\delta i}{vi}\cdot\frac{\delta\,(i+8)}{vi\,(i+8)} \qquad [1]$$

δ = average density of the ecological connection unit and corridors (ECUCOR) deriving from the UREN within the jth cell in the ith radial sector with j = 1;10 km and i = 1;8
v_i = standard deviation of the density values in the 10 cells for the ith radial sector

where: $$\delta i = \sum_{j=1}^{10} \frac{s_{ij}}{S} \qquad [2]$$

s_j = surface area of the ECUCOR present in the jth cell in the ith radial sector
S = surface area of the ith radial sector

The GE index returns the potential effectiveness of the gap in placing the two opposite sections of ecologically collaborating matrix in communication, while justifying on behalf of the Regional administration the financial investments for eco-engineering projects aimed at regenerating roadway underpasses to guarantee flows of land animals.
Of the 96 gaps examined, 44 had a good efficiency (mid, high, and very high) with respect to the surrounding presence of an ecologically "collaborating" matrix, that is, one that is capable of allowing the meaningful dispersion of land-animal fluxes in an appropriate environment. Figure 4 shows the relationship between gaps and the average quality of the UREN matrix, highlighting cases in which the gaps themselves allow for effective crossings as "ecological corridors". In these cases, there is heightened convenience for the regional entity to intervene with adequate protection and planning to guarantee the functionality of the bypass. This functionality holds particular importance in cases where systems of Natura 2000 Network SACs are present on the slopes of the infrastructure, for which the objective is to reduce ecological isolation. Some examples of this are shown in Figure 5.

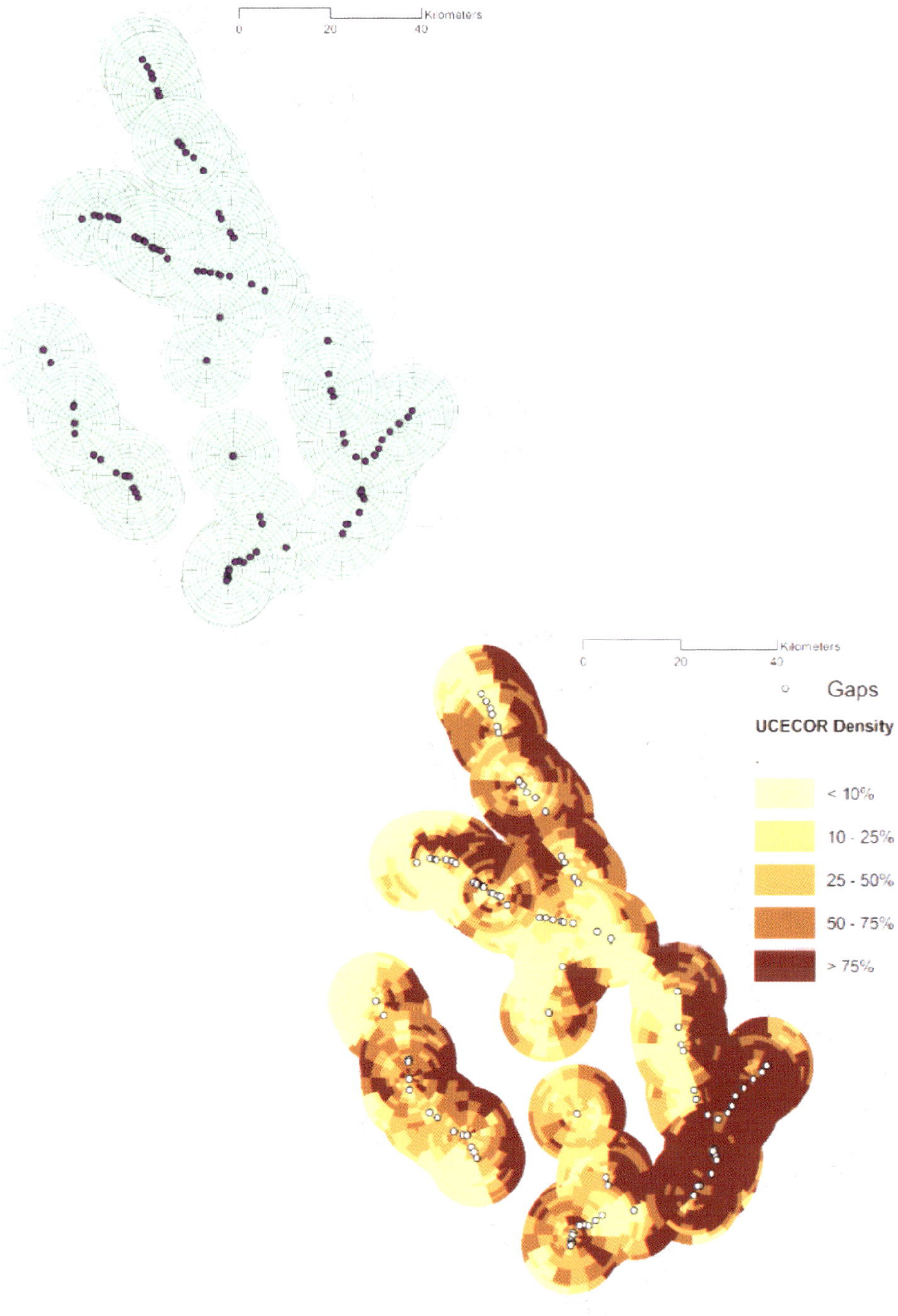

Fig.3 The radial grids centred on the gaps (a) and the ECUCOR density in the sectors and buffer zones (b)

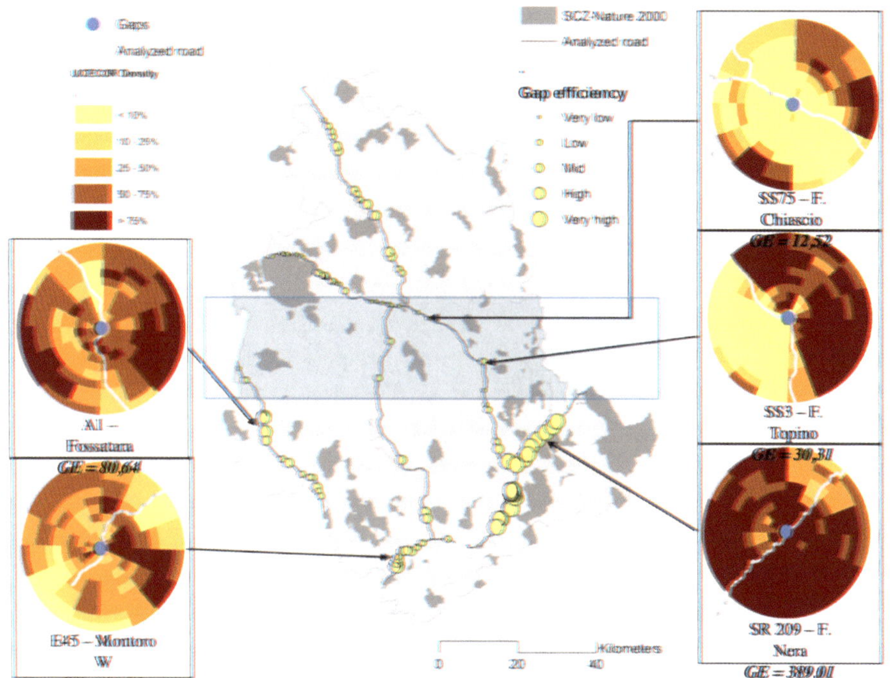

Fig.4 Sample of the values of the GE index and the geographical classification. In blue, the band lacking transverse bypasses of the infrastructure.

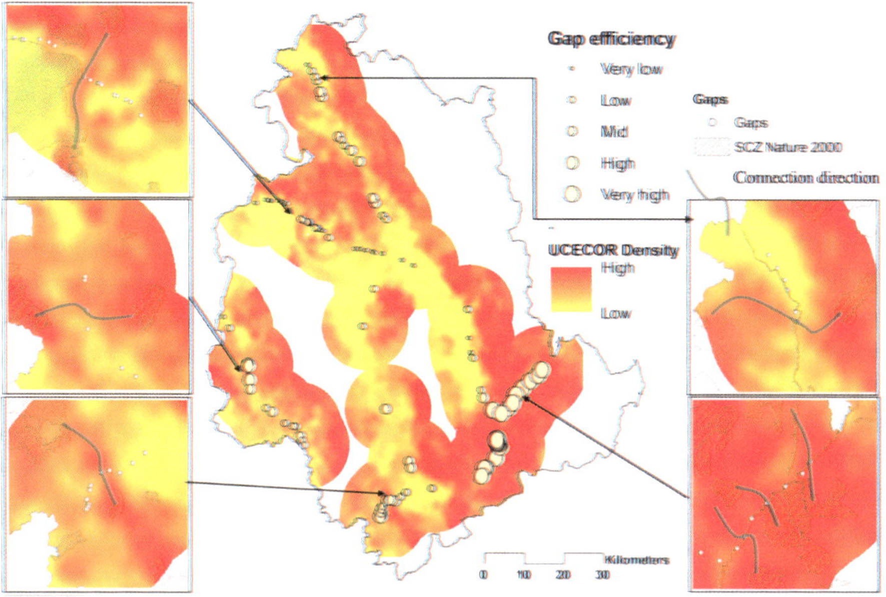

Fig.5 Geostatistical analysis of the density of the ECUCOR matrix and examples of preferential connection directions.

COM-AP Engagement of Comunanze to disseminate a self-sustainable model for agro-biodiversity conservation in the Apennine

Massimo Sargolini, Paolo Perna, Andrea Renzi

SAAD School of Architecture and Design – UNICAM University of Camerino

Livia Bellisari

Comunità Ambiente

Daniela Gigante, Fabio Maneli

DCBB, University of Perugia

The project entitled COM-AP Engagement of Comunanze to disseminate a self-sustainable model for agro-biodiversity conservation in the Apennines (LIFE18 GIE/IT/000840), developed under the LIFE Environmental Governance and Informationcall, was created with the goal of formulating a new management model of Natura 2000 Network sites based on the role and enhancement of local communities, which are characterized by being the territorial protection for the most fragile and marginal areas. According to results from the SUN LIFE project, the threats and pressures acting on the regional level are mainly represented by transformation processes regarding the management and abandonment of pastoral systems. The loss and damage of Habitat 6210 (*) are accompanied by various symptoms of deterioration (e.g., the invasion by shrub species and other competitive plant species), the impoverishment of fauna, the activation of erosive processes and land compacting, as well as the scarce availability of sources of water.

In addition, in Umbria, especially around Norcia, territorial transformations occurred following the earthquakes in 2016 and 2017 and these will continue to grow. In fact, following these events, there was an increase in the progressive process of depopulation already underway, with the consequent related acceleration of the loss of habitats and species that are very important for conservation and the landscape.

A diachronic cartographic analysis made by the UNIPG demonstrated that for a period of 8 years, the general reduction in surface area of Habitat 6210 (*) occurred mainly due to the lack of management. In Apennine sites, the annual rate of loss was estimated at an average of around 1.4%. Grasslands play an important social role from different points of view (production, recreation, conservation) and host many wild progenitors of cultivated species (Crop Wild Relatives), which are crucial for the protection of genetic biodiversity of food and to maintain the various uses (e.g., medicine, cosmetics) of spontaneous plant species. These are emblematic of the extraordinarily positive role that agriculture can play in conserving biodiversity and in the sustainable development of rural areas. For these reasons, it is undoubtedly clear that the abandonment of rural territories, with the consequent potential reduction of the grasslands, can have direct impacts on the state of biodiversity, in particular in sensitive areas such as the Apennines. Therefore, the Appenine territory as a whole can be delineated as important strategically for activating policies of sustainable development aimed at protecting the territory, local economic development, and therefore the protection of biodiversity.

In this perspective, a decisive element is the transformation of traditional jobs into new green jobs. Processes of business renewal and innovation and also the redefinition of educational plans for the growth of new young professionals to join the labour market therefore represent the points for investment in a strategic long-term vision.

These challenges constitute the basis for the proposal. With this project, the Umbria Region intends to involve itself with the agrarian communities (Comunanze) present around Norcia, in Campi in particular, to reinforce the role of local management and protection for the greater sustainability of practices to conserve biodiversity, through which a virtuous cycle of local development and progressive repopulation can be initiated.

More than 160 agrarian communities are present in the Umbria Region. These are subjects instituted with specific goals to protect the interests and rights of rural communities in guaranteeing the correct use and enhancement of the territory, preserving common goods through equitable and collective use.

The project aims to define a programme agreement within the community of Campi (City of Norcia), which represents an important example of marginal Apennine territory in which the levels of biodiversity are closely tied to maintaining the traditional management of the territory through agricultural practices, but in which it is the presence of humans itself that is at risk due to the destructive force of the earthquakes of 2016 and the consequent process of depopulation due to the inoperability of the houses and the unusability of the infrastructure and services.

The COM-AP project therefore addresses one of the priorities identified as urgent in the regional PAF within the SUN LIFE project, the results of which are testified to in this publication. The main objective is to develop a "platform" of knowledge and cooperation in order to raise awareness regarding the possible opportunities for agrarian communities, agricultural/ forest and pastoral companies, professional agricultural institutes, public institutions, and educational entities in developing concrete actions to locally implement the EU's directives aimed at protecting the natural and landscape heritage and adapting to the great economic and ecological changes underway.

The specific goals are:

1. Increasing the involvement of stakeholders and interested subjects, encouraging the community's proactive role, increasing knowledge and awareness with respect to:
   - the importance of operators in agriculture/forestry/shepherding in managing the Natura 2000 Network and the need to intervene with measures to conserve the species and habitats contained therein;

- the importance of species/habitats in the Natura 2000 Network, in particular 6210 (*);
   - the role and value of communities in maintaining the natural capital;
2. Integrating, transferring, and implementing knowledge with the scope of:
   - promoting sustainable development;
   - supporting the development of an ecosustainable production system and enhancing local characteristics (social, economic, environmental, cultural);
   - contrasting the progressive reduction in agriculture/forestry/shepherding activities in Natura 2000 Network sites, in particular those hit by the earthquakes in 2016;
3. Experimenting with good practices in the community of Campi (150 ha) as a virtuous model to promote, illustrate, transfer, and replicate to create a virtuous cycle of conservation of biodiversity and sustainable development in the Umbria Region;
4. Contrasting the loss of biodiversity through the development and adoption of sustainable behaviours and practices, but rooted in the traditional use and management of the territory;
5. Supporting the development of skills and professions in the green sector by involving companies and schools in common, integrated projects.

The main focus of the project will therefore be the local communities, which will be informed and educated in order to implement the best practices for sustainable agriculture, with continuous supervision and the support of technicians and experts. The COM-AP project will provide added value to management of the Natura 2000 Network in Umbria, developing a replicable, transferable model of sustainable management for rural areas.

References

- Cinquini F., Perna P., Sargolini M. (a cura di) (2006) Reti ecologiche e siti natura 2000, in Sargolini M., Cinquini F., Perna P. (a cura di) vol. 1, p. 1-223, Roma: Edizioni Kappa, ISBN: 9788878007423
- Sargolini M. (2007) La dimensione ecologica del paesaggio, in: Battisti C. e Romano B. Frammentazione e connettività. vol. 1, p. 376-379, Novara: de Agostini Scuola Spa, ISBN: 9788825173147
- Sargolini M. (2011) All'origine di tutto. Reti ecologiche nella pianificazione dei parchi e delle aree contigue, in: Falqui E., Calamita F. e Pavoni P. (a cura di) Paesaggio, luogo della mente. p. 541-566, pisa: edizioni ets, ISBN: 9788846730503
- Morandi F., Niccolini F., Sargolini M. (2012) Parks and Territory. New perspective in planning organization. p. 1-201, Barcellona: LISt lab Laboratorio Internazionala Editoriale, ISBN: 9788895623788
- Caprodossi R., Pierantoni I., Sargolini M. (2015) Reti ambientali, itinerari lauretani e comunità locali, in Marca/Marche, 4/2015; pp.: 99-114; Andrealivi Editore. ISSN:2284-0389
- Sargolini M. (2016) C'è un futuro per le aree protette? in: Moccia d., Sepe M., Reti e infrastrutture dei territori contemporanei. p. 187-197, Roma: Inu Edizioni, ISBN: 9788876031472

4

PROJECT MONITORING

Guidelines to the scientific monitoring of the network

Daniela Gigante, Enzo Goretti, Gianandrea La Porta, Massimo Lorenzoni, Fabio Maneli, Matteo Pallottini, Laura Pompei, Manuela Rebora, Roberto Venanzoni

DCBB, University of Perugia

Cristiano Spilinga, Francesca Montioni, Silvia Carletti, Emi Petruzzi

Studio Naturalistico Hyla

Among its main products, the SUN LIFE project includes a network of tools aimed at supporting the process of monitoring the state of conservation of species and Habitats in Directive 92/43/EEC presented in the Natura 2000 Network in Umbria, through the definition of species- and habitat-specific protocols optimized on the regional scale. The HD itself requires member states to activate these protocols, carry out surveillance activities, activate conservation measures, and assess their effectiveness. With DPR 357/1997, the responsibility for monitoring was assigned to the Regions.

From the methodological point of view, the guidelines adopted by the SUN LIFE project refer to the most consolidated scientific criteria developed in the sector of monitoring species, populations, and plant communities and habitats, also in consideration of European guidelines (Evans & Arvela 2012) and the indications contained in the "Manuals for monitoring species and habitats of European interest (Directive 92/43/EEC) in Italy" recently published by ISPRA with the support of scientific societies (Ercole et al. 2016; Stoch et al. 2016; Angelini et al. 2016) and some methodological contributions specifically dedicated to these themes (e.g., for the Habitats, Gigante et al. 2016b, 2016c). The standardized protocols, specific for Habitats and species, were also integrated based on the characteristics of the Natura 2000 Network in Umbria, taking account of local criticalities, intrinsic characteristics, and distributive specifics of the Habitats in Annex I, the species in Annexes II, IV, and V of the HD, and the species of birds in Annex I of the BD in the regional context, weighting them as well with reference to the general national and European framework.

With respect to the national protocols, further parameters were added that were useful for effective monitoring. In particular, for plant species and Habitats, specific information was inserted regarding: pressures and threats on the regional level (with reference to the official list IUCN-CMP Unified Classification v. 3.2-2011, deriving from Salafsky et al. 2008); phytosociological characterization of the Habitat on a regional level (Biondi et al., 2012);

methodological indications, both theoretical and practical, for the surveying and recognition of Habitats on a phytosociological basis (Dengler et al. 2008; Biondi 2011; Biondi et al. 2009, 2012, 2014; Biondi & Blasi, 2015); the distance from the series head, that is, the dynamic level reached by the representative plant community in the Habitat (or the biological habitat of a species) with respect to the potential natural vegetation that is current, known, or hypothesized for the station (Gigante et al. 2014), the expression of the greatest or least natural tendency to evolve, changing into a different community; the type of Habitat (or biological habitat) with reference to the model hat establishes three main types of spatial occupation in natural conditions: aerial, linear, or point-like (Gigante et al., 2016a); the regional values relative to the parameters to assess species and Habitats contained in the Standard Data Forms, averaged over the 102 Natura 2000 Network sites in Umbria; an expert-based evaluation of the level of rarity of the Habitat and species on a regional level, considering its effective known distribution.

For the 22 species of invertebrates, methods were proposed that largely repropose the indications for national protocols (Stoch & Genovesi, 2016), considering the changes necessary to adapt to the specifics of the regional context. In some cases, in addition, methodological variations were indicated that derived from the experimental activities being made on populations in the regional territory in order to estimate their size.

For fish, two common monitoring protocols were proposed for the 11 species and agnatha in Annex II present in Umbria, but differentiated for two types of environment: i) waterways that can be forded and ii) waterways that cannot be forded, lakes, and artificial bodies of water. In both protocols, qualitative and quantitative indicators were proposed that were useful for assessing the state of conservation of the species. These were based on national guidelines (Stoch & Genovesi 2016), as well as on what was proposed to implement the Water Directive 2000/60/EC in Italy (APAT 2007; ISPRA 2014; Volta et al. 2014).

For the 99 species of tetrapods (8 amphibians, 11 reptiles, 50 birds, and 30 mammals), monitoring methodologies were defined that repropose what was established on the national level (Stoch F., Genovesi P., 2016), considering the changes necessary for adaptation to the specifics of the regional context.

For the birds in the Directive, the monitoring protocols proposed were the fruit of a survey of what was already applied by the Regional Fauna Observatory, which has carried out monitoring throughout the regional territory for more than 20 years, optimizing the time and available resources.

With regard for the monitoring techniques, technical/operational indications were provided to perform the activities. For each Habitat and species, the parameters to consider, the related surveying techniques, and the optimal recommended surveying frequency were indicated. The methodologies proposed provide simple but effective procedures to collect uniform data based on shared principles and standardized techniques in order to provide information comparable on the local, regional, and national scales.

To complete the methodological aspects, a hierarchy of species and Habitats was developed in order to identify the real conservation emergencies on the regional scale. This was an indispensable tool for directing and planning monitoring activities appropriately and for using the resources, as well as for management interventions. Considerations regarding the ecology and biology of species and Habitats were integrated with an analysis of the state of conservation and anthropic pressures on a regional level, identifying and integrating metrics and indicators in order to provide a classification of conservation priorities. In the realization of an organic monitoring plan, the definition of priorities plays a key role in evaluating the appropriate methods and times to apply the various protocols. The considerations about priorities were made by dividing the regional territory into three homogeneous areas (large areas) that allowed for better implementation and quantification of the parameters considered to assess the conditions of species and Habitat conservation. These large areas represent uniform ecological spaces that, with respect to the division of the territory into biogeographical regions, allow for a finer reading of all the parameters considered. In particular, the regional territory was divided into wet zones, plain-hilly landscape, and Apennine landscape. Some of the main parameters on which the metrics were based to prioritize the Habitats were the following: Habitat priority as in Annex I; representativeness and rarity on the regional level, based on the potential natural vegetation (Biondi et al. 2010); real and potential presence of plant species from the Red List (Conti et al. 1997; Rossi et al. 2013); real and potential presence of plant species in Annex II; phytocenotic richness; risk of transformation for intrinsic reasons (plant succession); anthropic pressure; state of conservation on the national level from Report former Art. 17 (Genovesi et al. 2014). For the plant species, the most important parameters were the following: priority of species as in Annex II; IUCN degree of threat (Rossi et al., 2013); number of Natura 2000 Network sites with presence; level of knowledge; consistency of the regional population; number of stations regionally; vulnerability of the species' habitat. For the animal species, the monitoring priorities were based mainly on the degree of vulnerability (risk of extinction of the species nationally, in accordance with the categories defined by the IUCN Red List); vulnerability of the biological habitat (starting with the pressures and threats that affect the species); consistency of the populations; presence of Natura 2000 Network sites in the range of the species; degree of knowledge. An additional parameter was applied exclusively for the fish species in order to enhance the indigenous origin of the species in Umbria.

References

- Aa. Vv., 2014. Indirizzi E Protocolli Per Il Monitoraggio Dello Stato Di Conservazione Dei Chirotteri Nell'italia Settentrionale. Pubblicazione On Line: Http://Www.Centroregionalechirotteri.Org/
- Agnelli P., Martinoli A., Patriarca E., Russo D., Scaravelli D., Genovesi P., 2013. Linee Guida Per Il Monitoraggio Dei Chirotteri: Indicazioni Metodologiche Per Lo Studio E La Conservazione Dei Pipistrelli In Italia. Quad. Cons. Natura, 19, Mattm – Ist. Sup. Protezione E Ricerca Ambientale (Ispra), Roma.
- Angelini P., Casella L., Grignetti A., Genovesi P., 2016. Manuali per il monitoraggio di specie e habitat di interesse comunitario (Direttiva 92/43/CEE) in Italia: habitat. ISPRA, Serie Manuali e Linee Guida, 142/2016.
- APAT, 2007. Protocollo di campionamento e analisi della fauna ittica dei sistemi lotici. In: Metodi Biologici per le Acque. Parte I. Manuali e Linee Guida, APAT, Roma, 31 pp.
- Biondi E., 2011. Phytosociology today: Methodological and conceptual evolution, Plant Biosystems, 145 (1): 19-29.
- Biondi E., Blasi C., Allegrezza M., et al. 2014. Plant communities of Italy: The Vegetation Prodrome. Plant Biosystems, 148(4): 728-814.
- Biondi E., Blasi C., 2015. Prodromo della Vegetazione Italiana. MATTM. http://www.prodromo-vegetazione-italia.org/
- Biondi E, Gigante D., Pignattelli S., Rampiconi E., Venanzoni R., 2010. Le Serie di Vegetazione della Regione Umbria. In: Blasi C. (Ed.) La Vegetazione d'Italia: 257-279. Palombi & Partner S.r.l. Roma. ISBN: 978-88-6060-290-9
- Biondi E., Blasi C., Burrascano S., Casavecchia S., Copiz R., Del Vico E., Galdenzi D., Gigante D., Lasen C., Spampinato G., Venanzoni R., Zivkovic, 2009. Manuale Italiano di Interpretazione degli habitat della Direttiva 92/43/CEE. SBI, MATTM, DPN. Available at http://vnr.unipg.it/habitat/index.jsp.
- Biondi E., Burrascano S., Casavecchia S., Copiz R., Del Vico E., Galdenzi D., Gigante D., Lasen C., Spampinato G., Venanzoni R., Zivkovic L. & Blasi C., 2012. Diagnosis and syntaxonomic interpretation of Annex I Habitats (Dir. 92/43/ EEC) in Italy at the alliance level. Plant Sociology, 49(1): 5-37.
- Bologna M. A., La Posta S., 2004. Monitoring the conservation status of threatened amphibian and reptile species of Italian fauna. Italian Journal of Zoology n.71.
- Conti, F., A. Manzi, e F. Pedrotti. 1997. Liste Rosse Regionali delle Piante d'Italia. WWF Italia, Società Botanica Italiana, CIAS, Univ. Camerino. 139 pp.
- Dengler J., Chytrý M., Ewald J., 2008. Phytosociology. In: Jørgensen S.E. & Fath B.D., (Eds.-in-Chief), General Ecology. Vol. 4 of Encyclopedia of Ecology, 5 vols. pp. 2767-2779. Oxford: Elsevier.
- Ercole S., Giacanelli V., Bacchetta G., Fenu G., Genovesi P. (Eds.), 2016. Manuali per il monitoraggio di specie e habitat di interesse comunitario (Direttiva 92/43/CEE) in Italia: specie vegetali. ISPRA, Serie Manuali e linee guida, 140/2016.
- Evans D., Arvela M., 2011. Assessment and reporting under Article 17 of the Habitats Directive. Explanatory Notes & Guidelines for the period 2007-2012. Final version. July 2011. ETC-BD.

- Genovesi P., Angelini P., Bianchi E., Dupré E., Ercole S., Giacanelli V., Ronchi F., Stoch F., 2014. Specie e habitat di interesse comunitario in Italia: distribuzione, stato di conservazione e trend. ISPRA, Serie Rapporti, 194/2014.
- Gigante D., Foggi B., Venanzoni R., Viciani D., Buffa G., 2016a. Habitats on the grid: The spatial dimension does matter for red-listing. Journal for Nature Conservation, 32: 1–9.
- Gigante D., Attorre F., Venanzoni R., 2016b. Box 3: Note metodologiche ai protocolli di monitoraggio. In: Angelini P., Casella L., Grignetti A., Genovesi P. (Eds.), Manuali per il monitoraggio di specie e habitat di interesse comunitario (Direttiva 92/43/CEE) in Italia: habitat. ISPRA, Serie Manuali e Linee Guida, 142/2016: 12-14.
- Gigante D., Attorre F., Venanzoni R., et al., 2016c. A methodological protocol for Annex I Habitats monitoring: the contribution of Vegetation science. Plant Sociology, 53(2): 77-87. doi: 10.7338/pls2016532/06.
- Gigante D., Maneli F., Venanzoni R., 2014. The role of Potential Natural Vegetation for Rete Natura 2000 Habitat monitoring. Plant Sociology, 51(1): 137-147.
- ISPRA, 2014: Protocollo di campionamento e analisi della fauna ittica dei sistemi lotici guadabili. Manuali e linee guida, ISPRA, Roma,111: 20 pp.
- Rossi G., Montagnani C., Gargano D., Peruzzi L., Abeli T., Ravera S., Cogoni A., Fenu G., Magrini S., Gennai M., Foggi B., Wagensommer R.P., Venturella G., Blasi C., Raimondo F.M., Orsenigo S. (Eds.), 2013. Lista Rossa della Flora Italiana. 1. Policy Species e altre specie minacciate. Comitato Italiano IUCN e Ministero dell'Ambiente e della Tutela del Territorio e del Mare.
- Salafsky N., Salzer D., Stattersfield A.J., Hilton-Taylor C., Neugarten R., Butchart S.H.M., Collen B., Cox N., Master L.L., O'Connor S., Wilkie D., 2008. A Standard Lexicon for Biodiversity Conservation: Unified Classifications of Threats and Actions. Conservation Biology, 22(4): 897–911.
- Stoch F., Genovesi P. (Eds.), 2016. Manuali per il monitoraggio di specie e habitat di interesse comunitario (Direttiva 92/43/CEE) in Italia: specie animali. ISPRA, Serie Manuali e linee guida, 141/2016.
- Velatta F., Lombardi G., Sergiacomi U., Viali P., 2009. Monitoraggio dell'Avifauna umbra. Trend e distribuzione ambientale delle specie comuni. I Quaderni dell'Osservatorio. Regione Umbria
- Velatta F., Muzzatti M., Montefameglio M., Chiappini M.M., 2010 - Monitoraggio di alcune specie di Ardeidi coloniali nidificanti al Lago Trasimeno - Riv.ital. Orn., 80 (2): 95 – 103
- Volponi S., 2003. Progetto Italiano Sforzo Costante. Sintesi della stagione di attività 2002. PRISCO Bollettino n. 1. Centro Nazionale di Inanellamento, Istituto Nazionale per la Fauna Selvatica, Ozzano Emilia (BO).
- Volta P., 2013. Indice per l'analisi dello stato di qualità della fauna ittica finalizzato alla valutazione dello stato ecologico dei laghi italiani: Lake Fish Index (LFI). In: Indici per la valutazione della qualità ecologica dei Laghi. Report CNR-ISE, 02.13, 115-138.

5
COMMUNICATION OF THE PROJECT

5.1

Communication of the SUN LIFE

Cristiano Spilinga, Francesca Montioni, Silvia Carletti, Emi Petruzzi

Studio Naturalistico Hyla

Actions for dissemination play an extremely important role, considering that one criticism connected to the Natura 2000 Network today is precisely the public's lack of knowledge about it.

For this reason, when drafting the project, as established by the LIFE programme, these activities were carried out starting in the initial phases in order to seek useful involvement not only to publicize the project and the Natura 2000 Network, but also for participation in realizing the content itself.

The main objective of the communication actions was therefore to spread greater knowledge and awareness about the Natura 2000 Network as the result of an indirect communication campaign directed at various targets: the general public, stakeholders, schools, and the media.

To ensure that this goal would be reached, direct, participatory communication was used on the level of the local communities affected by Natura 2000 Network areas, activating and involving local administrations, citizen associations, and others that represent economic interests in the territory.

Another important aspect was raising awareness in the regional public opinion, which represents a strategic element for the spread not only of knowledge about the heritage represented by the Natura 2000 Network, but also to attribute general value to its existence.

Dissemination activities, like the materials used in support of it, were differentiated according to the target groups of reference.

To raise awareness in the public opinion and with citizens in general, an informational brochure about the project was produced and distributed at events and demonstrations. The informational brochure about the Natura 2000 Network and the Z-Card contain a synthetic description about the Natura 2000 Network in Umbria and a map with the location of the various sites.

In addition, a guide to the Natura 2000 Network sites was created, which invites visitors to the Special Areas of Conservation and the Special Protection Areas, as well as their natural characteristics, using the regional trekking network as a connective element.

For the stakeholders, specific products were created, such as the "Guidelines for farmers and foresters to conserve biodiversity in the Natura 2000 Network". The guides aim to illustrate the role of agriculture and forestry in the Natura 2000 Network in Umbria, and to provide the main users of agricultural and forest resources in the Region with information and advice for the optimal management of activities from a sustainable point of view.

In addition, a path was taken to involve stakeholders in a participatory process that, through territorial interactions, would lead to full sharing in both the "Guidelines for farmers and foresters to conserve biodiversity in the Natura 2000 Network" and the "Strategy for managing the Natura 2000 Network in Umbria".

As well, dissemination activities aimed at the technical public were also performed and organized by the partner universities thanks to participation at congresses and conferences and the publication of scientific articles.

Specifically for schools, numerous awareness-raising activities were carried out. Infodays were organized for presentation to teachers in the Scoprinatura Contest, a competition about raising environmental awareness open to students and teachers from all primary and secondary schools present in the Umbria Region. In the contest, students symbolically adopted a Natura 2000 Network site in Umbria and created a work or initiative to communicate and promote the site itself. The winning classes were awarded with trips to the Natura 2000 Network sites.

For teachers, educational seminars were organized to learn about the SUN LIFE project, the Natura 2000 Network, and the biodiversity contained in the sites in Umbria. Edukits were experimented with at the seminars. These were designed as a tool to invite students to deepen their knowledge about the Natura 2000 Network in Umbria through an A3-sized poster to hang in the classroom and the Scoprinatura game. In the game, the dynamics of the classic game "Snakes and Ladders" is changed, guiding students along a path that leads through all the regional compartments identified (high Tiber Valley, Apennines, high and low Valnerina, Orvieto, Trasimeno, and other valleys in Umbria) and touches the Natura 2000 Network sites in the Region. The Edukit was distributed to 100 classes where the project was presented, and it was used to carry out awareness-raising actions on themes related to the Natura 2000 Network.

For the media, a press kit was created and provided on a pen drive that contained, in addition to the logos and the slogan designed for the communication campaign, a .pdf version of the brochure, a summary of the project, press releases, a series of photos, and a video. Within the project, a video was created that simply and immediately allows the greater public to understand the biodiversity protected by sites in the Natura 2000 Network in the Region. The press kit was distributed to news offices at events where the project was presented and will also be distributed during the final conference.

To enable the greatest dissemination of the project, press releases were periodically sent to the Umbria Region press office and articles were written about the project that appeared widely in daily, weekly, and monthly newspapers and webzines.

As with the press, some tools such as the website and Facebook page allowed all targets to be reached. The objectives of the website were twofold. Firstly, it served to provide information about the SUN LIFE project and its objectives, actions, etc., and to reinforce the spread of design products. Secondly, it became the focus for disseminating the tools for the communication campaign and therefore the spread of knowledge and information about the Natura 2000 Network in Umbria. The website was continually updated with regard to the activities thanks to the activation and management of the Facebook page, which reached the expected number of visitors.

SUN LIFE
Strategy for managing the Natura 2000 Network in Umbria

Edited by
Paolo Perna, Ilenia Pierantoni,
Andrea Renzi, Massimo Sargolini

Editorial Director
Alessandro Franceschini

Published by
LISt Lab
info@listlab.eu
listlab.eu

Art Director & Production
Blacklist Creative, BCN
blacklist-creative.com

ISBN 9788899854331

**Printed and bound
in the European Union,**
September 2018

serie 

Promotion and distribution in Italy
Messaggerie Libri, Spa, Milano,
assistenza.ordini@meli.it;
amministrazione.vendite@meli.it

International promotion and distribution
ACC Book Distribution Ltd
Woodbridge, Suffolk, IP12 4SD, UK
sales@antique-acc.com

LISt Lab is an editorial workshop, based in Europe, that works on contemporary issues. LISt Lab not only publishes, but also researches, proposes, promotes, produces, creates networks.

LISt Lab is a green company committed to respect the environment. Paper, ink, glues and all processings come from short supply chains and aim at limiting pollution. The print run of books and magazines is based on consumption patterns, thus preventing waste of paper and surpluses. LISt Lab aims at the responsibility of the authors and markets, towards the knowledge of a new publishing culture based on resource management.